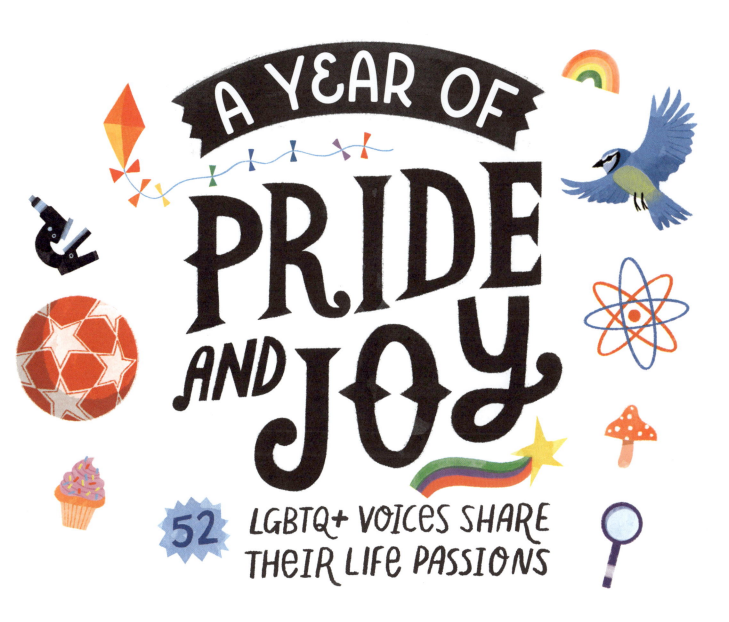

A YEAR OF PRIDE AND JOY

52 LGBTQ+ VOICES SHARE THEIR LIFE PASSIONS

curated by
SIMON JAMES GREEN

illustrated by
RUTH BURROWS

MAGIC CAT PUBLISHING
NEW YORK

CONTENTS

JANUARY

8

The Joy of Bird-Watching
Actor Rebecca Root
National Bird Day

10

The Joy of Flowers
Florist Paul Hawkins
International Flower Day

12

The Joy of Learning
Educator and Historian Blair Imani
International Day of Education

14

The Joy of Magic
Magician Nathan Jones
International Magicians' Day

FEBRUARY

16

The Joy of Wetlands
Artist James Aldridge
International Wetlands Day

18

The Joy of Old Films
Actor Stephen Fry
Global Movie Day

20

The Joy of Experiments
Material Scientist Dr. Clara Barker
International Day of Women and Girls in Science

22

The Joy of Radio
Radio and Podcast Host Rob Gillett
World Radio Day

MARCH

24

The Joy of Scorpions
Curator of Arachnology Lauren Esposito
World Wildlife Day

26

The Joy of Action
Politician James Roesener
World Advocacy Day

28
The Joy of Fantasy Books
Embarrassing Bodies' Dr. Anand Patel
World Book Day

30
The Joy of Words
Magazine Publisher Darren Styles
National Word Day

32
The Joy of Theater
Director AeJay Antonis Marquis
World Theater Day

 APRIL

34
The Joy of Well-Being
LGBTQ+ Healthcare Activist Dr. Jo Hartland
World Health Day

36
The Joy of Pets
Singer Rina Sawayama
National Pet Day

38
The Joy of Dancing
Presenter Dr. Ranj Singh
International Dance Day

40
The Joy of Helping Animals
Veterinarian Abby McElroy
World Veterinary Day

42
The Joy of Writing with Pride
Writer Matt Cain
National Tell a Story Day

 MAY

44
The Joy of Eurovision
Teacher Andrew Moffat
Eurovision Song Contest

46
The Joy of Family
Lawyer Nancy Kelley
International Family Equality Day

48
The Joy of Noticing
Farmer Hannah Breckbill
National Garden Meditation Day

50
The Joy of Driving Trains
Train Driver Romolo Lanzi
National Train Day

52
The Joy of Cracking Cases
Detective Thomas Williams
Sherlock Holmes Day

JUNE

54
The Joy of Community
Well-Being Officer Dòmhnall Idris
LGBT Pride Month

56
The Joy of Protecting Our Planet
Writer and Editor Matthew Todd
World Environment Day

58
The Joy of Knitting
Olympic Diver Tom Daley
World Knit in Public Day

60
The Joy of Fairies
Writer and Actor Amelia Gann
International Fairy Day

JULY

62
The Joy of Laughter
Comedian Julian Clary
International Joke Day

64
The Joy of Making Jam
Paulus the Cabaret Geek
National Jam Day

66
The Joy of Drag
Showbiz Star and *Strictly Come Dancing* Judge Craig Revel Horwood
International Drag Day

68
The Joy of a Team
Soccer Player Joanie Evans
International Day of Friendship

AUGUST

70
The Joy of Play
YouTuber and Author Calum McSwiggan
National Playday

72
The Joy of Hand-Lettering
Designer Jae Lin
World Calligraphy Day

74
The Joy of My Dog
Casting Director Robert Sterne
National Dog Day

76
The Joy of a Beach Walk
Charity Executive Mark Russell
National Beach Day

SEPTEMBER

78
The Joy of Indian Cinema
Actor Seyan Sarvan
National Cinema Day

80
The Joy of Small Moments
Entrepreneur Kortney Ziegler
World Gratitude Day

82
The Joy of Drawing Comics
Cartoonist Lewis Hancox
National Comic Book Day

84
The Joy of Cooking
Theatrical Producer Cameron Mackintosh
National Cooking Day

OCTOBER

86
The Joy of Teaching
Teacher Patty Nicolari
World Teachers' Day

88
The Joy of Fungi
Environmentalist Isaias Hernandez
National Mushroom Day

90
The Joy of Food
Actor Miriam Margolyes
World Food Day

92
The Joy of Restoration
Singer-Songwriter Will Young
International Repair Day

94
The Joy of Swimming
Actor Emma D'Arcy
World Swim Day

NOVEMBER

96
The Joy of Scientific Discovery
Scientist Biswajit Paul
National STEM Day

98
The Joy of Urban Hiking
Professor Myeshia Price
National Hiking Day

100
The Joy of Making Shows
Director Amy Coop
World Television Day

102
The Joy of Drawing
Illustrator Ruth Burrows
National Illustration Day

DECEMBER

104
The Joy of Soccer
Politician Mhairi Black
World Football (Soccer) Day

106
The Joy of Pantomime
Pantomime Dame Mama G
World Panto Day

108
The Joy of Basketball
Basketball Player Abby Dunkin
World Basketball Day

110
The Joy of Paws
Singer-Songwriter Chet Lam
Christmas

Dear Reader,
What is joy?

It's more than just happiness. Joy is something deeper, which comes from within us. It gives us a sense of purpose and meaning, sparks pleasure, and makes life worth living. What you'll find as you dip into this book is that joy takes many forms. From kicking a soccer ball and traveling to new places, to spending time with family or appreciating the beauty of nature, joy comes in all shapes and sizes, and can be found everywhere.

The world can feel like a scary place sometimes—especially if you're made to feel like an outsider because of who you are. But in these pages, you'll find 52 LGBTQ+ folk from all walks of life and from many different countries, cultures, and backgrounds, and they're all living rich, joyful lives.

If you want to be inspired by brilliant people and their fascinating lives, pick up this book. If you're looking for a new hobby or skill to try, pick up this book. If you're going through a tough time, and you just need to know it's going to be OK, and that the world is full of love and light, then please, pick up this book. And I hope you find your joy, too.

With love and joy,
Simon James Green
Author

NATIONAL BIRD DAY

THE JOY OF BIRD-WATCHING

Actor Rebecca Root

My garden teems with birds that eat, drink, play, bathe, and sleep.

One spring morning, I was working at my desk overlooking the garden. I heard the whirring of wings and grabbed my binoculars. A female house sparrow had landed on my bird feeder and began pecking at the seeds. She was alert and agile, clinging upside down to the wires with her feet. She was soon joined by another house sparrow, a male this time (you could tell by the markings), and they dined side by side.

Watching birds takes me into the wildness of their world.

Then, a juvenile sparrow flew in, followed by another, then a third. They perched on the birch tree, squealing expectantly. They opened their mouths hungrily to their parent, who duly delivered morsels to the gaping beaks. I see this behavior daily, but it is no less hypnotic. Watching birds takes me into the wildness of their world, helping me reconnect with the planet, and all the beautiful creatures we share it with.

INTERNATIONAL FLOWER DAY

THE JOY OF FLOWERS

Florist Paul Hawkins

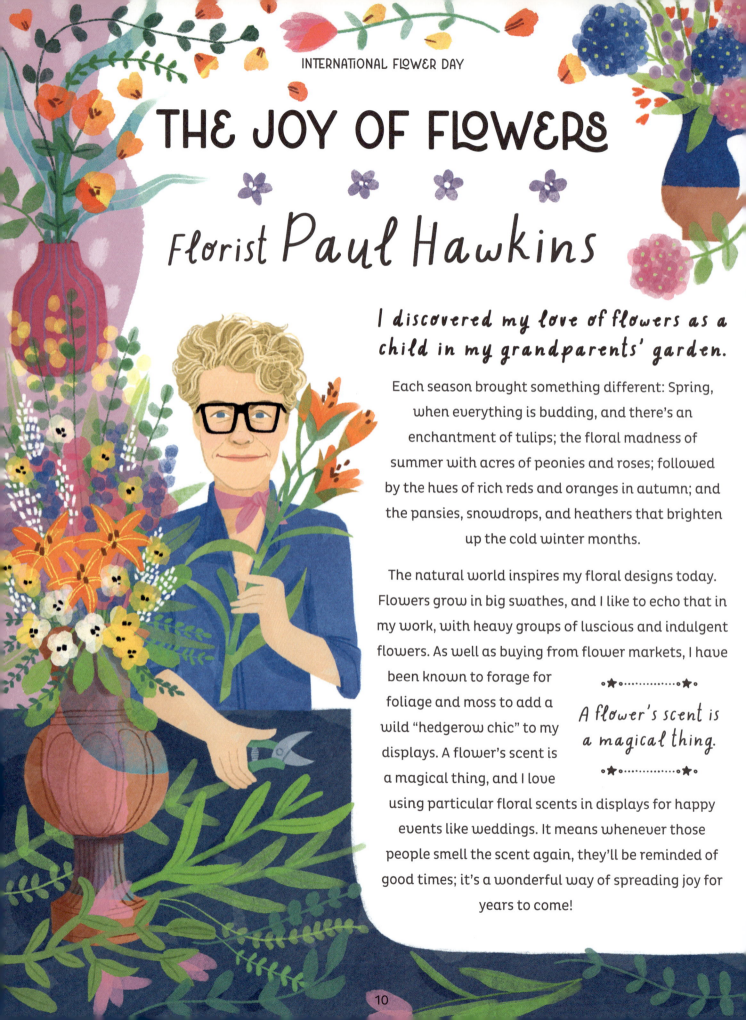

I discovered my love of flowers as a child in my grandparents' garden.

Each season brought something different: Spring, when everything is budding, and there's an enchantment of tulips; the floral madness of summer with acres of peonies and roses; followed by the hues of rich reds and oranges in autumn; and the pansies, snowdrops, and heathers that brighten up the cold winter months.

The natural world inspires my floral designs today. Flowers grow in big swathes, and I like to echo that in my work, with heavy groups of luscious and indulgent flowers. As well as buying from flower markets, I have been known to forage for foliage and moss to add a wild "hedgerow chic" to my displays. A flower's scent is a magical thing, and I love using particular floral scents in displays for happy events like weddings. It means whenever those people smell the scent again, they'll be reminded of good times; it's a wonderful way of spreading joy for years to come!

A flower's scent is a magical thing.

INTERNATIONAL DAY OF EDUCATION

THE JOY OF LEARNING

Educator and Historian Blair Imani

Growing up, I never felt like I was "smart."

Having attention deficit hyperactivity disorder (ADHD) made it difficult to focus, and my dyslexia sometimes made it harder for me to spell words correctly. I found myself getting frustrated for taking longer on tests than my classmates. But now that I'm grown up, I recognize intelligence comes in many forms. It might take me a little longer, but I eventually get it right. And even though reading and writing is still difficult for me, I'm proud to say that I've written three books.

As an educator and historian, I encourage everyone to learn new things, even when it might be a challenge. Learning new information is one of the most exciting parts of being alive. We can learn new words that help us better understand ourselves and we can learn new ideas that help us show love and respect to the people in our lives.

Learning new information is one of the most exciting parts of being alive.

Blair's Reasons to Learn Something New

There are lots of benefits to educating yourself and trying new things. Here are just four of them!

IT WILL GIVE YOU CONFIDENCE
Whether it's memorizing your times tables or a short poem, learning a new skill can increase confidence and boost your self-esteem.

IT'S GOOD FOR YOUR HEALTH
Learning a new skill can give you a mental and physical boost. It's exercise for the brain, and your brain ages just like you do, so it's important to look after it.

YOU WILL BETTER UNDERSTAND YOURSELF
Learning new things isn't just important for school or work, it's also important for ourselves. Learning about the world around you can help you find what you are passionate about, help you face your fears, and help you become more compassionate and creative.

IT CAN HELP YOU SOLVE PROBLEMS
Life is full of challenges and sometimes we run into problems that need solutions. Being curious and practicing your critical thinking skills can help you overcome many of life's challenges.

JANUARY

INTERNATIONAL MAGICIANS' DAY

THE JOY OF MAGIC

Magician Nathan Jones

I will never forget the joy I felt watching magic for the first time.

I was eight years old when a performer from a local circus stood right in front of me and vanished a paper napkin into thin air! I felt the hairs stand up on the back of my neck, and for a second nothing else mattered. I had to know how it was done! The kindest thing that performer did was not to tell me. The magic is in the mystery.

I am lucky enough to travel the world and perform magic of my own now. The pleasure I get in passing on that joy to other people is something I cherish. People often say to me, "Magic isn't real though, is it? It's just tricks!" But I think magic is that feeling you get when you see something impossible happen right in front of your eyes and it fills you with wonder. And for me that's very real.

> The magic is in the mystery.

Nathan's Vanishing Coin Magic Trick

This was the very first magic trick I learned, almost 25 years ago. Once you've mastered this trick, you'll be the talk of the town . . . if you're not already!

WHAT YOU'LL NEED:

- A shiny coin
- A clear drinking glass
- Two matching sheets of paper
- A glue stick
- Scissors

THE SECRET TO THIS TRICK
Ahead of time you must carefully cut and glue a piece of paper to the mouth of the glass. This should be the same size as the opening.

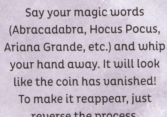

Place the glass on the matching piece of paper (next to the coin) and you're ready to perform. Simply wrap your fingers around the bottom of the glass and move the glass to cover the coin.

Say your magic words (Abracadabra, Hocus Pocus, Ariana Grande, etc.) and whip your hand away. It will look like the coin has vanished! To make it reappear, just reverse the process.

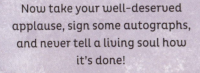

Now take your well-deserved applause, sign some autographs, and never tell a living soul how it's done!

JANUARY

INTERNATIONAL WETLANDS DAY

THE JOY OF WETLANDS

Artist James Aldridge

I feel calm and happy when I spend time in wetlands, walking alongside a river or watching the life that lives in a marshy pond.

When I was a child, I used to spend hours by my grandmother's two ponds, waiting for frog faces to poke up between the plants, or turning over lily pads to find pond snails and their slippery clusters of eggs. I was almost fifty before I got a pond of my own, dug with my son and husband one Easter weekend, but it didn't take long for the water striders and diving beetles to arrive.

As an artist, a lot of my work happens by rivers—drawing and taking photos or making films. Rivers give us so much—the water we drink, somewhere to paddle or swim, a way to travel—and they don't always receive the love they deserve in return. But the river keeps on flowing, bringing life and joy to us and all the other animals that depend on it.

I feel calm and happy when I spend time in wetlands.

James's Guide to Wetlands and Well-Being

Making artwork helps me to slow down and notice what's around me. It fills up my cup with joy. Here are a few ideas you might like to try, too:

OPEN YOUR EYES TO LOCAL WETLANDS

What wetlands are near you? A river? A canal? A pond? What shapes can you see on the water's surface?

Try **DRAWING** some of the shapes. Let your hand move like water, flowing across the page. If you have paint, let it run and ripple.

LOOK FOR THE WILDLIFE

What wildlife lives in your local wetlands? Dragonflies? Ducks? A salamander? Don't worry if you don't know their names, our senses can tell us so much.

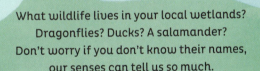

Use a list of **DESCRIPTIVE WORDS** or a simple poem to describe how an insect moves, or the colors and patterns on a duck's feathers. Try to mimic the sound of birds singing or the wind in the reeds.

TAKE A MOMENT TO RECORD WHAT YOU NOTICE

I use sketchbooks to record what I notice. Perhaps you could start a river journal?

Using a book that you've made (a few pieces of paper joined together with a stapler) or one that you've bought, continue with the writing and drawing you started above. Add a **RUBBING OF LEAVES** or tree bark and stick in the natural treasures that you find.

GLOBAL MOVIE DAY

THE JOY OF OLD FILMS
Actor Stephen Fry

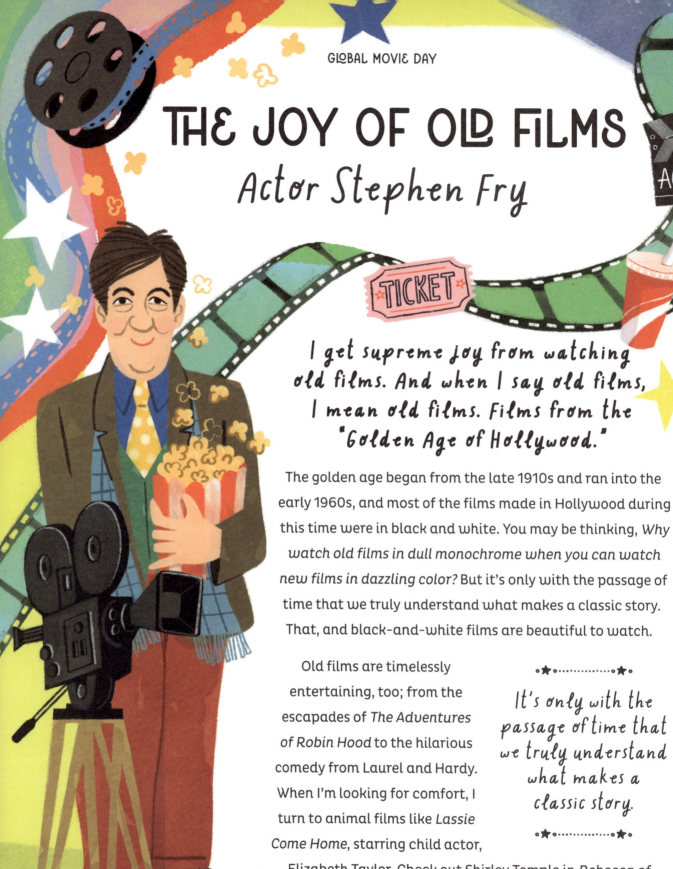

I get supreme joy from watching old films. And when I say old films, I mean old films. Films from the "Golden Age of Hollywood."

The golden age began from the late 1910s and ran into the early 1960s, and most of the films made in Hollywood during this time were in black and white. You may be thinking, *Why watch old films in dull monochrome when you can watch new films in dazzling color?* But it's only with the passage of time that we truly understand what makes a classic story. That, and black-and-white films are beautiful to watch.

Old films are timelessly entertaining, too; from the escapades of *The Adventures of Robin Hood* to the hilarious comedy from Laurel and Hardy. When I'm looking for comfort, I turn to animal films like *Lassie Come Home*, starring child actor, Elizabeth Taylor. Check out Shirley Temple in *Rebecca of Sunnybrook Farm*, too. And then there's . . . oh, I've gone on long enough. Dive in and don't be afraid of black and white!

It's only with the passage of time that we truly understand what makes a classic story.

Stephen's Film Club

Films are one of the best forms of entertainment because they offer something for everyone. Here are just a few of my favorite films:

LAUREL AND HARDY
Released: 1921–1951

Starring in 106 films, this iconic British-American comedy duo were legends. Perfect for people who love a physical type of comedy known as slapstick . . . I mean, who doesn't love people crashing into things?!

THE WIZARD OF OZ
Released: 1939

This magical film tells the story of Dorothy and her dog, Toto, who are swept away by a tornado to the Land of Oz. There they meet a scarecrow, a tin man, and a lion, and travel to the Emerald City to see the Wizard of Oz.

LASSIE COME HOME
Released: 1943

This film was the first in a series of seven films starring "Lassie," a loyal collie, who is sold to a rich duke by her less well-off family. Lassie escapes from the duke's home in Scotland and begins a tough trek back to her home in Yorkshire, facing many perils along the way.

THE RED BALLOON
Released: 1956

A wordless French film about a little boy and a red helium-filled balloon. The balloon seems to have a mind of its own and follows the boy even though his mother does not let it into their house. Filmed in post-war Paris, the balloon becomes a symbol of hope for a better future.

FEBRUARY

INTERNATIONAL DAY OF WOMEN AND GIRLS IN SCIENCE

THE JOY OF EXPERIMENTS

Material Scientist Dr. Clara Barker

I enjoy spending time in my laboratory.

The world of science is fascinating, and plasmas are my favorite thing to create. You may know that ice, water, and steam are all water—but in the form of solid, liquid, and gas. But there is another state called plasma. If you see the glow around lightning when it strikes, that is a plasma.

My team and I make new materials (particularly superconductors) with plasmas. We use metal boxes (chambers) with all the air removed, then use electricity and magnets, with gases like argon and oxygen, to help us to break the metals into tiny parts called atoms and ions. Because the atoms and ions have high energy, they release light and, depending on which metal and gas we use, we can get different colors. Plasma may not be the most conventional state of matter, but it's remarkable and provides an important contribution, which is symbolic of the LGBTQ+ community. Maybe that's why I love it so much!

> The world of science is fascinating.

Producing Electricity with Dr. Clara

There are lots of different ways to make electricity, and as a society we are moving toward ways that are more friendly to our planet. You may have heard of solar power or seen wind turbines. Another way is called fusion.

With FUSION, we make two really small particles smash together. This is hard because, like magnets with the same polarity, they want to push each other apart. But if we can make them join together, they release a lot of energy. This is exactly what the sun does, and even though it is a long way away, we can feel the heat on Earth!

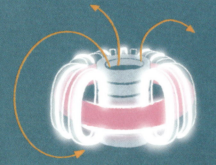

One machine that can do this is called a TOKAMAK. In order for fusion to occur, these particles that want to repel must crash into each other, which we can force using strong magnetic fields.

When the particles collide into each other, they form a PLASMA that produces a temperature of over 270 million degrees Fahrenheit that we can change into electricity.

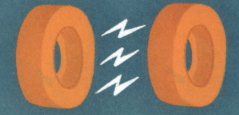

We use SUPERCONDUCTING MAGNETS to squeeze the particles together to force them to join. This keeps the really hot plasma away from the walls of the Tokamak.

It is very hard, but if we make it work, we can produce lots of energy (like mini suns on Earth!) to power our homes in a safe way that is GOOD FOR THE ENVIRONMENT.

FEBRUARY

WORLD RADIO DAY

THE JOY OF RADIO

Radio and Podcast Host Rob Gillett

I discovered the joy of radio at the age of three.

The joy arrived during a week-long power outage that left us with a battery-powered radio as the only entertainment. The pop songs and DJ's voice combined inside that black box to become something magical.

Growing up, radio and I were inseparable. I got my first radio job as a reporter in Brighton, UK, before going on to do the news on the morning show. It was a huge privilege to meet so many different people and bring their stories to life on air. In 2020 I launched *Queerly*, an LGBTQ+ radio station. Even now, every time I reach for the mic I still feel a sense of joy and disbelief that I get to be that voice inside the radio.

> I still feel a sense of joy and disbelief that I get to be that voice inside the radio.

Rob's Guide to Creating Your Own Show

Everything you need to create your own radio show or podcast is built into the average smartphone or laptop. Here are some tips to creating your own show:

PICK A TOPIC YOU ARE PASSIONATE ABOUT
For me it was always music, but for you it might be sports or science—or even the latest TV show everyone at school is watching!

RECORD YOURSELF SPEAKING
It will help you get used to how you sound and understand how your voice works. When people can't see you, your voice is all you have to convey the emotions that are usually communicated by your face.

PRACTICE INTERVIEWING
You could involve your friends as co-hosts or ask a family member or teacher to appear as a guest. Hit record and go for it! Mistakes will happen, it's how you deal with them that counts.

GET PERMISSION
Always make sure you ask a parent or guardian before broadcasting yourself or sharing a recording and most important of all, have fun!

FEBRUARY

WORLD WILDLIFE DAY

THE JOY OF SCORPIONS
Curator of Arachnology
Lauren Esposito

Growing up I loved flipping over rocks and storing found insects in egg cartons.

It didn't occur to me that I might eventually become a scorpion scientist! I spent a lot of time as a child with my family on the beach. My grandparents lived on a tiny island in the Bahamas, called Elbow Cay, which had crystalline turquoise water and a blindingly white sandy beach.

We often played a game where we would find the tiniest, most perfect shell among the grains of sand. I could spend hours playing this game because it always felt like no matter how tiny of a shell you could find, there was always something more tiny or more beautiful. Just like those little shells, there are scorpions out there ... but you have to really look for them due to their secretive nature. Even today, I can spend hours looking through the leaves on the ground and find joy in all of the tiny critters, some no bigger than a grain of sand!

There are scorpions out there ... but you have to really look for them!

Lauren's Scorpion Fact File

Did you know scorpions have been around since before the age of the dinosaurs?

COMMON NAME: Scorpions

SCIENTIFIC NAME: Scorpiones
TYPE: Invertbrates
DIET: Carnivore
AVERAGE LIFE SPAN IN THE WILD: 2 to 20 years
SIZE: 3 to 9 inches

SCORPIONS ARE ARTHROPODS, and are closely related to spiders. They have eight legs, but it may look like they have six because two of them act as PINCERS.

Scorpions can be spotted by the venomous STINGER at the end of their curled tails.

SCORPIONS ARE REALLY GOOD MOMS! They don't lay eggs but instead give birth to baby scorpions called scorpionlings, which they carry around on their back for up to a month or two after they are born.

SCORPIONS ARE PREDATORS and eat other animals, mostly things that are active at night like moths and crickets. This is because scorpions are NOCTURNAL, or active mostly at night. During the day scorpions sleep in holes that they dig in the soil or between rocks, called burrows.

MARCH

WORLD ADVOCACY DAY

THE JOY OF ACTION
Politician James Roesener

I have been drawn to advocating for justice all my life.

In 2022 I became the first openly trans man elected to a state legislature in U.S. history. I see change and growth as an opportunity to make the world a better place. I surround myself with people who are not afraid to share their thoughts in a loving way so that we can collaborate and make something great together.

That we can all fight for equal rights in our own way brings me the greatest joy. Every person is important. Whether you draw some art showcasing diverse families, write a story about making a stand against discrimination, or be part of a sports team that has rainbow laces on their boots, the world will always benefit from more people using what they love to do to showcase unity and fight for equality.

> That we can all fight for equal rights in our own way brings me the greatest joy.

James's Justice Trailblazers

There are lots of people around the world advocating for justice and equal rights. These are just some people and groups who are fighting to level up.

GEORGINIO WIJNALDUM
Dutch soccer player Georginio wore a captain's armband bearing the words "One Love" and a rainbow motif during UEFA Euro 2020. He said, "The armband means a lot because I STAND FOR DIVERSITY—one love means everybody is a part of it, and everybody should be free to be who they are."

CHARLIE AMAYA SCOTT
A trans-femme advocate of Navajo heritage, Charlie is an advocate among Indigenous people and beyond. She uses her Instagram account to explore the concept of TWO SPIRIT, an Indigenous term that describes a person with both a masculine and feminine spirit.

CIEARA WEST AND CLAIRE GREILLER
Cieara and Claire set up ENVIRONMENTAL QUEERS, a nonprofit that brings together Los Angeles-based queer people with a shared love of the environment. They plan environmentally friendly events for their community, such as beach cleanups and tree plantings.

PETER TATCHELL
Peter Tatchell helped organize Britain's first gay pride march in 1972. Since then, he has campaigned on many issues and has been director of the Peter Tatchell Foundation since 2011, a nonprofit organization which seeks to PROTECT HUMAN RIGHTS.

Think about what you enjoy doing and how you could use that passion to help fight for equal rights.

WORLD BOOK DAY

THE JOY OF FANTASY BOOKS

'Embarrassing Bodies' Dr. Anand Patel

At the age of twelve, I picked up a book called Dragonriders of Pern.

The plot was about a boy who didn't fit in, who loved dragons. That was me, I thought! I escaped into a different world where the unique, the abandoned, the lonely got to be heroes. I have been devoted to fantasy novels ever since.

I think some people look down on fantasy novels, but I see a jump into the unknown for someone who's scared to jump; the most imaginative stories for someone who needs a little break from reality. These books aren't empty, they're full of life and excitement, and importantly, a sense of fairness, honor, and justice. While there might be significant ups and downs on the way, the main character usually wins out. For a child who felt he had no power and couldn't change the way he or the world was, I found my happy place. These books gave me peace and joy, and I still return to the world of Pern when I need a rest from the world today.

Fantasy books are full of life and excitement

Dr. Anand's Fantasy Creature Creator

A fantasy creature is an imagined being. Here are my top tips for creating your own that you could include in a fantasy story!

DECIDE WHAT YOUR CREATURE LOOKS LIKE. A good trick is to mix and match human, animal, and sea creature elements to create something new. How about a dog . . . with wings? Or a snake with a shark's head?

GIVE IT A MAGIC POWER. Does it have super strength? Does it breathe fire? Can it shoot lightning bolts out of its tusks?

GIVE IT A HOME. Does your creature live alone up in space or with a group of others in a forest? Or perhaps underground in the ocean!

GIVE IT A NAME. A good source of fantasy creature names is to look for Latin or Greek words. The Latin word for *fierce* is *ferox*, and that could be a great name for a scary creature!

GIVE IT A PURPOSE. Is the creature there to protect precious treasure? Or does it prefer to cause mischief? Is it good or evil?

Once you've worked these elements out, you're ready to write your creature story!

NATIONAL WORD DAY

THE JOY OF WORDS
Magazine Publisher Darren Styles

Aren't words wonderful things? Tiny, precision instruments.

As a young kid I felt different, even if I didn't have the body of words to describe how. Looking back I know I was special. There wasn't another me, not anywhere. And even if I didn't fit in yet, I found company in books, with words, and my imagination fired. I could do anything, be anyone, I could become a storyteller. I found joy in words. I could explain how I felt, who I was. I learned to say I was a boy who liked boys because I'd learned that was OK.

As the publisher and owner of *Attitude*, a British gay lifestyle magazine, the words I share now as an adult, written down or spoken, can change lives. I can educate, inform, entertain, and—sometimes, if I'm lucky—inspire others to do the same. And if you enjoy what you do, there is always joy within. Which, if you look carefully, is a play on words!

> I found joy in words. I could explain how I felt, who I was.

Darren's Favorite Words

Aren't words amazing? Here are some of my favorite words.

KAYAK
Kayak is a PALINDROME, a word that reads the same backward as forward. Like peep or wow. Which is pretty cool.

DISCOMBOBULATION
A hard word to read, an even harder word to say. It means a feeling of confusion that leaves you feeling uneasy.

ORANGE
Because nothing in the world rhymes with orange. You will now spend ten minutes trying to prove me wrong. Good luck with that.

PLOP
I love a word that sounds like the thing it's describing. Like *pop* or *bang*. That's called ONOMATOPOEIA!

PORTMANTEAU
Pronounced port-man-toe, meaning two words combined as one. Like spoon + fork = spork. Or iPod + broadcast = podcast. Create your own!

SCURRYFUNGE
When mom or dad say clean your room, and you haven't, and you hear them coming up the stairs, so you rush around picking things up, you are scurryfunging!

WORLD THEATER DAY

THE JOY OF THEATER

Director AeJay Antonis Marquis

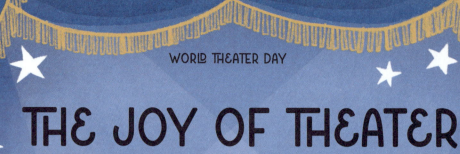

When I think about the theater, I think about possibilities.

The theater is a blank canvas, and a stage holds so much freedom within its embrace. Actors stand on the stage, projecting words from passionate prophets, poets, and philosophers, and the theater becomes an escape from the real world. It is a place where everyone is different, and yet they are united under a single production.

When we feel overwhelmed or worried about the real world, the theater invites us to process this with strangers who quickly become friends. When I listen to Nina Simone's song, *I Wish I Knew How It Would Feel to Be Free*, I think about the theater and lay my burdens on the stage. My freedom and my dreams. That's what the theater means to me. Do you want to come dream of liberated worlds with me? I'll meet you on the stage.

> The theater is a place where everyone is different, and yet they are united under a single production.

AeJay's Spotlight on Stages

Imagine a world of pretend, but where the stage itself changes the story!
Theater comes alive in many shapes and sizes. Let's peek behind the curtain:

PROSCENIUM
This stage has a fancy frame, like a giant painting! It's perfect for grand sets and big casts, just like seeing a story come to life in a magical box.

ROUND
The audience surrounds the actors in this circular space. It's like being right in the middle of the action, making you feel part of the adventure!

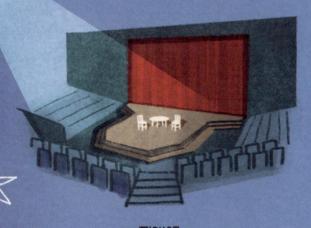

THRUST
Imagine a stage that juts out like a handshake. The audience sits on two or three sides, creating a closer, more personal experience.

BLACK BOX
This flexible space has black walls, ready for any kind of story. It's like a blank canvas for imagination, with lighting and sets creating endless possibilities!

WORLD AS A STAGE
This theater isn't in a building at all! It could be a park, a museum, even a street. The performance uses the real world as its set, making the story come alive in surprising ways.

MARCH

WORLD HEALTH DAY

THE JOY OF WELL-BEING

LGBTQ+ Healthcare Activist Dr. Jo Hartland

Well-being looks different for everyone because no two people are the same.

It might be the way our bodies are shaped, how we move, how we think, or even how we dress. Sometimes people will tell you being different is a bad thing. I want you to remember this isn't true. I am loved for being the unique and precious individual I am. And you are, too.

I am proud that I am different. I am pansexual, (which means I'm attracted to people regardless of their sex or gender), gender queer (I ask people to use they, them or their to describe me instead of he, him or his), and disabled. Embracing my differences helps me know what I need to feel well and look after myself. I stay happy by talking about my mental health. I set boundaries with the people around me. I wear clothes that make me smile. I want everyone to celebrate all the different ways we can feel well . . . we all deserve to feel good!

We all deserve to feel good!

Dr. Jo's Guide to Well-Being

What can you do to keep yourself feeling well?
I like to:

STAY ACTIVE
There are lots of different ways we can exercise to make our body and mind feel good! The most important thing is to find something you enjoy. Remember, if you feel too tired or your body hurts it's OK to take a break.

LOOK AFTER MY MENTAL HEALTH
Our emotions are an important part of our health, but we don't always have to feel happy. Sometimes it's OK to feel sad, angry, or worried. When we feel like this it's important to talk about it with people we trust.

GET ENOUGH SLEEP
Sleep is important for our bodies and our brains. When sleep is difficult check your:

- Screen time—try to put down your phone or tablet and pick up a book

- Diet—avoid too much sugar or caffeine as it can keep us awake

- Emotions—tell someone if you are in pain or feeling anxious before bed

SET BOUNDARIES
A boundary might be: "I only want a hug when I ask for one" or "I don't like people touching my hair without asking me." Boundaries are important for our whole body, and if you feel worried or scared that someone isn't listening to your boundaries then tell a trusted adult.

NATIONAL PET DAY

THE JOY OF PETS
Singer Rina Sawayama

Pets are scientifically proven to be good for you.

Being around them, cuddling them, or taking them on walks have been shown to have positive effects on people's mental health. Pets don't judge people based on their race, age, gender identity, or sexuality. They love unconditionally as long as you care for them.

Different pets suit different people—you just need to find the right one for you! Ever since I can remember I have loved having a pet dog. Big ones, little ones, cute ones, scruffy ones.

> *Ever since I can remember I have loved having a pet dog.*

I now have a pet Staffordshire bull terrier named Kaya, and when I'm going through a tough time, I cuddle her and everything is OK. With her permanent staffy smile and long caramel tail (that's always wagging!) she reminds me that we are all worthy of unconditional love. Pets teach us what's really important in life and help us focus on the small daily joys around us.

Rina's Guide to Choosing the Right Pet

Pets bring a lot of joy to our lives, but it's important to properly research what pet might suit you best. Here are some thoughts to get you started:

There are many breeds of DOG, and choosing the right one is important. Herding dogs are known for being intelligent and can be easily trained but need lots of exercise. Terriers are energetic but can be stubborn.

CATS are affectionate and make good companions, while also being quite independent. They do need space to be active though, as well as access to a litter box that needs to be cleaned regularly.

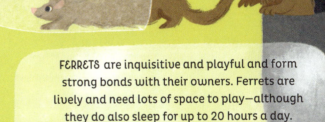

RABBITS come in different shapes and sizes. Your bunny will need a safe living space with room to hop, run, and jump, and enough straw to keep them warm.

FERRETS are inquisitive and playful and form strong bonds with their owners. Ferrets are lively and need lots of space to play—although they do also sleep for up to 20 hours a day.

FISH are beautiful and are relaxing to watch, but can be challenging to keep as they have complex needs. Aquariums can be expensive as they require filters, heating, and lighting, and have to be constantly maintained.

HAMSTERS are adorable, but nocturnal! (They're active at night and may not be up when you are.) They're full of energy and love to explore. To keep them happy, provide a spacious cage with plenty of hiding spots, a wheel to run on, and safe chew toys.

APRIL

INTERNATIONAL DANCE DAY

THE JOY OF DANCING
Presenter Dr. Ranj Singh

When life gives you lemons, DANCE!

A couple of years ago, I made myself a promise: No matter what was going on in my life, or in the world, I would always try to find my joy. And then I discovered that there are so many different things that bring me it. Belting out my favorite songs at karaoke, going for a hike through the hills with my friends, playing dinosaurs with my nephews, or going to see a musical. All these things make my face beam with happiness.

But there is one thing that never fails to lift me up. One thing I always came back to. And that is dancing. When I was invited to be a dancer on the BBC One dance series *Strictly Come Dancing*, I jumped at the chance! Moving to music is my therapy, my medicine. If I'm feeling down, I'll get up and go dancing. If I'm anxious, I'll move and work the feelings out. For me, dancing is joy made manifest. It's magic.

> *Moving to music is my therapy, my medicine.*

Dr. Ranj's Joyful Dances

I dazzled on the *Strictly* dance floor in 2018—and learned the moves to some of the most energetic and fun dances. Want to try?

In a WALTZ, two people dance in elegant circles while holding each other. There is always one person who leads, and the other follows.

The CHA-CHA is a fast ballroom dance of Latin American origin. It has a basic pattern of three steps and a shuffle.

The QUICKSTEP is very fast! It requires a lot of energy and the ability to dance lightly and gracefully on your feet; the best quickstep dancers often appear as if their feet barely touch the ground.

DISCO is a fast-paced dance with lots of movement. One of the easiest moves is the "bump." Sway your hips from left to right with the beat and time your movement with a partner so you gently bump hips every other beat.

There are many variations of the TANGO. The Argentinian version is where two people hold each other closely, walk quickly in one direction, then walk quickly back again.

APRIL

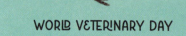

WORLD VETERINARY DAY

THE JOY OF HELPING ANIMALS

Veterinarian Abby McElroy

As a veterinarian, I have the privilege of helping sick animals feel better.

It's much like when you get sick and visit a doctor to feel better. However, there's a unique challenge in veterinary care—our patients can't verbally communicate their problems. We must act like detectives, investigating symptoms and behaviors to uncover the root cause of their illness.

My job fills me with immense joy because by healing hurt animals, I provide comfort to the people who cherish these creatures as their best friends. It's a gratifying journey that connects my passion for animals with my dedication to helping their human companions. Every day as a veterinarian is an adventure, and it's a privilege to be part of the intricate tapestry of their lives, nurturing their well-being and strengthening the bonds between pets and their people.

> By healing hurt animals, I provide comfort to the people who cherish these creatures as their best friends.

A Day in the Life of Abby

A day in my life as a veterinarian is a fulfilling mix of compassion and responsibility.

It begins early, with me REVIEWING PATIENT RECORDS. The clinic soon bustles with activity as pets and their anxious owners stream in seeking care.

My mornings are often dedicated to ROUTINE CHECKUPS and VACCINATIONS. But in this profession, there's always room for the unexpected. URGENT CALLS might summon me to a critical case—a dog injured in an accident, or a cat suddenly taken ill. These moments put my skills and decision-making to the test!

Midday sees me in the operating room PERFORMING SURGERIES ranging from spaying and neutering to intricate procedures. Afternoons are a flurry of interpreting lab results, updating concerned pet owners, and making vital treatment choices.

As the day winds down, PAPERWORK AWAITS—charts to update, invoices to send. It's a little boring, but the knowledge that I've eased suffering, and the joy of reuniting pets with grateful owners, keeps me going (along with a cup of tea and slice of cake!).

APRIL

NATIONAL TELL A STORY DAY

THE JOY OF WRITING WITH PRIDE

Writer Matt Cain

I find joy when I write stories that celebrate the LGBTQ+ community.

When I was growing up in northern England in the 1980s, I was bullied for not fitting in with the other boys, and then for being gay. It got so bad at one point that I didn't know how I could carry on. I certainly didn't think that one day I'd be an author writing about queer people like me—or that so many people would want to read my books.

Even though it was difficult at the time, I can see that the pain I went through has made me a better writer. Not only did it give me the drive to prove myself, but it also gave me the depth of feeling you need to write. I write characters who've felt similar things to me, put them in situations I've experienced, and show how they eventually succeed and find happiness. I've turned the negativity into something positive, something joyful, and something I'm proud of. Sometimes overcoming the challenges life throws at you can be the making of you. And one day it may even be the source of your queer joy!

> *I've turned the negativity into something positive, something joyful and something I'm proud of.*

Matt's Tips for Writing with Pride

If you're going through a difficult time, creating a fictional world can be a way of coping.

INVENT A CHARACTER
Start with easy things like their name, age, and what they look like.

Then ask more difficult questions: What is their favorite food? If they had three wishes, what would they be? What is a secret they've never told anybody?

GIVE YOUR CHARACTER A PROBLEM
Every story needs a problem for your character to overcome. You could base this on your own experiences—just like I did!

Think about anything in your life that made you unhappy or stressed—a family pet dying, or a big test at school, for example. Now give that problem to your character!

HOW WILL THEY SOLVE IT?
Now think about all the ways they could overcome that problem.

Is it something a friend or family member could help with? Or does it require your character to face their fears alone, be brave, and show the world who they really are?

INCLUDE A HAPPY ENDING!
Everyone likes a story where a character finds joy—it reminds us that we all deserve happiness and even when life gets tough, better days are usually just around the corner.

Make sure you know your happy ending before you even start your story—if you don't know where your character is going to end up, you won't know how to get them there!

Don't worry about showing anyone your work at first. Put your story to one side for a few days and come back to it with fresh eyes—this way you can be your own editor.

EUROVISION SONG CONTEST

THE JOY OF EUROVISION

Teacher Andrew Moffat

The Eurovision song contest is a year-round source of joy for me.

I first watched Eurovision in 1981, as a nine-year-old, and all through the 80s never talked about it to anyone. At the time Eurovision was thought to be "cheesy" and "uncool" . . . it sounds funny to say that now as it's an event that is increasingly loved and celebrated.

Today, most of my friends are born from a love of Eurovision; it's a shared passion that brings joy to all of us.

I go to the contest every year and see people that I only meet during that one week in May, in a different city somewhere in Europe.

Eurovision brings different people and cultures together in a wonderful way.

As well as the jaw-dropping sets, intricate choreography, and stunning fashion, Eurovision brings different people and cultures together in a wonderful way. What could be more joyful than that, I ask you?!

Andrew's Eurovision Party

Held annually in a different European city, Eurovision began as a way of uniting countries after World War II. It now includes 40 countries—and you can even take part at home since it's available on some streaming services.

Eurovision is an international songwriting competition in which each participating country picks a song and an artist or group to perform it live.

Eurovision is the perfect excuse for DRESSING UP—glitter, feather boas, disco outfits . . . the more over-the-top and outrageous the better!

Assign each guest a country and ask them to bring some REGIONAL FOOD from that place. Hopefully, you'll end up with some delicious French cheese, German bratwurst, Italian pizza, and British pork pies. Yum!

Make a list of all the countries and give them a SCORE after watching their performance based on the performer, dancing and wow factor. Will your choice be the same country that's crowned winner at the end of the contest?!

MAY

INTERNATIONAL FAMILY EQUALITY DAY

THE JOY OF FAMILY
Lawyer Nancy Kelley

My family makes my heart SING, especially my two little boys.

Like many LGBTQ+ people, my wife and I didn't grow up assuming we'd be moms. But ten years ago, we had the chance to adopt our eldest son, and our boys have been lighting up our lives ever since. When they were babies, I loved singing them to sleep, playing at the sand and water playground, or just watching them make a mess! These days, they tease me about being bad at gaming (I am!), and we spend our time walking the dogs and watching movies together. They may be growing up, but I still sing them to sleep every night.

Families aren't just things you are born into; they are things you build. Our family is made up of all kinds of incredible people: Some are from the families we were born into, others we have met in our path through life. All families are precious in their own ways, and full of joy. I hope your chosen family brings you joy, too.

All families are precious in their own ways, and full of joy!

Nancy's History of LGBTQ+ Parenting

Lots of LGBTQ+ people are parents, but until quite recently, the law didn't protect our families. Families were being broken apart because many people thought LGBTQ+ people shouldn't be allowed to raise children.

ADOPTING CHILDREN

Until recently, it was illegal for most same-sex couples to adopt a child in the United States. Many state laws dictated that only married couples could adopt, and marriage was not legal for LGBTQ+ couples in most states.

In 2015, a SUPREME COURT RULING made same-sex marriage legal in all 50 states, paving the way for same-sex couples to adopt—making families like mine possible.

HAVING CHILDREN

LGBTQ+ parents can build a family in all kinds of ways.

As well as adoption, there's also FERTILITY TREATMENT SUCH AS IVF, which is when an egg is fertilized with sperm in a laboratory and then returned to the womb to grow and develop, and SURROGACY, which is when a person agrees to carry and give birth to a baby for someone else.

When we do this, our families are recognized and protected in law, though this is still not as straightforward as it is for parents who are not LGBTQ+.

RAINBOW FAMILIES

The term *rainbow family* refers to a family with parents of the same sex bringing up a child, or an LGBTQ+ parented family.

As time goes by, more and more people feel able to come out as LGBTQ+ and live their lives to the fullest.

Every one of those people is someone's child, and many of them will grow up to parent in a new generation of BEAUTIFUL, JOYFUL RAINBOW FAMILIES.

MAY

NATIONAL GARDEN MEDITATION DAY

THE JOY OF NOTICING

Farmer Hannah Breckbill

By noticing things, I appreciate things.

I am a farmer at Humble Hands, where we grow vegetables and raise sheep. I work outside no matter the weather, and I try to notice something new every day. Sometimes I notice the wildlife, like the fat bluebird I saw on a crisp autumn day perched on top of a tall sunflower. Sometimes I notice the ways plants are growing—like the way the cabbages swell, almost to bursting this year! And sometimes I notice a sensation in my body, like the tired feeling of a hard day's graft.

Noticing helps me feel connected to the world around me. As it turns out, the small joys in our lives, like observing the size of bluebirds or the swell of a cabbage, sometimes turn out to be the most important. As humans we have a small part to play in this vast universe, and it is a joy to stop and appreciate the changes around me with gratitude.

> *Noticing helps me feel connected to the world around me.*

48

Hannah's Growing Guide

Humble Hands is a farm located in Decorah, Iowa. You don't need to own a farm to grow food, though. Here are some things you could try to grow where you live:

HERBS LIKE CRESS
Cress is quick and easy to grow indoors. Simply sow a packet of cress seeds onto some damp paper towels in a saucer on a windowsill. Spray with water to keep damp. They'll be ready to harvest in 5-8 days. Delicious on an egg salad sandwich!

OR HERBS LIKE CHIVES, MINT, PARSLEY, AND SAGE!
You don't even need a garden; you can grow herbs in a window box! Make sure the box has drainage holes, use good quality potting mix, and place it in a sunny spot.

VEGETABLES
A vegetable patch in your garden is great, but you can also grow vegetables in window boxes. Crops like lettuce, carrots, beets, and parsnips are particularly easy, and the seeds can be sown directly where they are going to grow between March and May. Scatter seeds evenly over the area (or plant in neat rows), cover lightly with soil, and water.

MAY

NATIONAL TRAIN DAY

THE JOY OF DRIVING TRAINS

Train Driver Romolo Lanzi

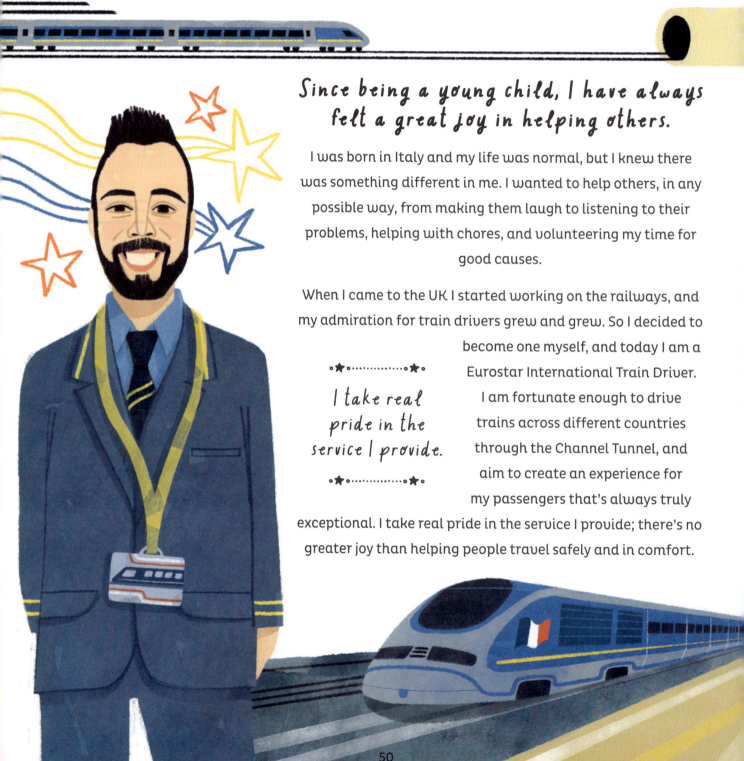

> Since being a young child, I have always felt a great joy in helping others.

I was born in Italy and my life was normal, but I knew there was something different in me. I wanted to help others, in any possible way, from making them laugh to listening to their problems, helping with chores, and volunteering my time for good causes.

When I came to the UK I started working on the railways, and my admiration for train drivers grew and grew. So I decided to become one myself, and today I am a Eurostar International Train Driver. I am fortunate enough to drive trains across different countries through the Channel Tunnel, and aim to create an experience for my passengers that's always truly exceptional. I take real pride in the service I provide; there's no greater joy than helping people travel safely and in comfort.

I take real pride in the service I provide.

Romolo's Channel Tunnel Facts

The Channel Tunnel opened in May 1994 and connected Great Britain with France. It has since been named one of the seven wonders of the modern world.

It took six years to build and, at nearly 24 miles, is the LONGEST UNDERSEA TUNNEL IN THE WORLD.

The tunnel is estimated to have cost $15 BILLION TO BUILD.

ELEVEN TUNNEL BORING MACHINES (TBMS) were used to dig the tunnels. These huge machines would cut through the chalk, collect the debris, and transport it behind using conveyor belts. This would then be hauled up to the surface using railroad wagons. The earth that was dug out could fill a sports stadium seven times!

More than 13,000 PEOPLE, from engineers to technicians, were employed to construct its three tunnels.

The tunnels merge at two points under the sea where the trains change line. These CROSSOVERS are tall enough to stand three double decker buses on top of each other!

MAY

The excavated earth came from the CRETACEOUS PERIOD—a time when dinosaurs walked the Earth!

The Channel Tunnel contains THREE TUNNELS running parallel to each other. Between the two railway tunnels is a third, smaller tunnel which is mainly used by maintenance workers.

51

THE JOY OF CRACKING CASES
Detective Thomas Williams

The story of Sherlock Holmes fascinated me as a child.

Sherlock Holmes was a detective. He used his intelligence and observation skills to solve cases—and often helped people along the way. I knew I wanted to become a detective to help people, too. And I knew it from the age of eight years old when I took on my most challenging investigation: Who made suspicious marks on my grandparents' floor?

Growing up, my cousin and I often spent time at my Nan and Pa's house. One Saturday after my grandparents had a new floor laid, it was quickly discovered that damage had been caused. I put my detective hat on and spoke to the people who had been in the kitchen. I made a list of who had seen what—to allow me to identify any motives.

As I pondered who it could be, I tilted back on the kitchen chair I was sitting on to help me think... and as the legs scraped against the floor I realized it was me! I was the culprit! The challenge of putting the puzzle together to establish the correct outcome was such a thrill that I've never looked back.

> *I knew I wanted to become a detective to help people.*

Thomas's Detective Tips

Could you be the next Sherlock Holmes?

DRESS LIKE A DETECTIVE
Choose clothes that help you to blend in and allow you to move around unnoticed. Don't forget your magnifying glass!

RECORD THE CLUES
Every detective needs a notebook—you never know when you'll need to refer to who said what to help you solve the crime. Don't forget your pen to write with!

GET A SIDEKICK
Choose a good sidekick to help you along the way—whether that's your pet dog or your best friend. After all, two brains are better than one!

MAKE YOUR BADGE
You'll need to show your badge when you're conducting official business. You can make a detective badge out of paper or cardboard. It should have your name and the name of your detective agency on it.

SET UP YOUR FINGERPRINTING KIT
A big part of detective work is gathering fingerprints. Get flour or baby powder, a paintbrush, and some clear tape to collect prints.

MAY

LGBT PRIDE MONTH

THE JOY OF COMMUNITY

Well-Being Officer Dòmhnall Idris

Growing up is an adventure. You'll journey to various places and meet some fascinating people who are just as curious about you as you are about them.

But perhaps most of all, you'll find yourself in a group with some of these amazing, lovely people, and that's the beauty of community. Every day in a community is cause for celebration. There's an undeniable aura of joy and togetherness in the air. And when challenges emerge, a community bands together, much like a family bound by love and understanding.

As an LGBTQ+ Muslim, I wanted a community where I could learn and practice Islam without hiding my sexual identity. My community is one where every person is cherished and welcomed. It's a haven where differences are not just tolerated but embraced, and where kindness reigns supreme. Ultimately, it's the joy of community that infuses my life with its enchantment, filling my heart with love, laughter, and the promise of a brighter tomorrow.

> Every day in a community is cause for celebration.

Dòmhnall's Community Scavenger Hunt

A community is more than just a gathering of people; it's a warm embrace, a sanctuary where everyone's uniqueness is celebrated. Head outside and search for yours today.

WHAT YOU NEED
- Paper or notebook
- Pen or pencil
- Chalk

Explore the place you live with a friend or family member.

Look for signs of community: Can you find a library, perhaps, or a food bank? Write each one down on your list.

Get creative! For places without a name (like spotting a friendly neighbor watering plants), draw a picture.

After your hunt, discuss what you found. How do these places and activities help people in your community?

If you have chalk draw a giant heart on the pavement and write "Our Community" inside (Make sure you get permission!).

Can you think of any other ways your community helps each other?

Next time, focus on a specific part of your community, like a local shop or annual festival. How does it make your neighborhood special?

As you do, remember every person adds unique threads to the tapestry of a community.

JUNE

WORLD ENVIRONMENT DAY

THE JOY OF PROTECTING OUR PLANET

Writer and Editor Matthew Todd

My journey toward environmental activism began when I united with like-minded individuals.

Discovering the depth of pollution and the looming threat of climate change initially left me feeling disheartened. While I had dedicated most of my life to advocating for LGBTQ+ rights, I soon realized that the health of our planet transcends all other identities. Clean air, clean water, and a thriving Earth are fundamental necessities for every living being, regardless of our backgrounds or beliefs.

This shared commitment to healing our planet has given me a profound sense of fulfilment.

The enormity of the environmental crisis can be daunting, but standing alongside fellow activists, I feel a sense of purpose and empowerment. This shared commitment to healing our planet has given me a profound sense of fulfilment. There's no better feeling than knowing that, as part of a united front, I am actively contributing to safeguarding the future of our world. In the end, it's a joy that transcends individual identity, for a healthier planet benefits us all.

Matthew's Path to Becoming an Environmental Activist

Becoming an environmental activist is a wonderful way to instill a sense of responsibility for our planet. Here's how you can do it:

LEARN ABOUT THE WORLD
The first step in becoming an environmental activist is to understand the issues. Read books, watch documentaries, and explore websites. When you see how magical this world is—from incredible insects to powerful polar bears to wondrous waterfalls, and tons more—you'll want to protect it, too!

JOIN OTHERS
Participate in local environmental initiatives. This could involve joining a community cleanup event, planting trees, or helping with a neighborhood garden. Working with others in their community will give you a sense of purpose and show you that your actions can make a positive impact.

SPREAD AWARENESS
Kids often get left out of lots of important discussions, but it's your world, too. Make your parents, teachers, and other grown-ups—and even politicians like the president or prime minister (who you can write to)—know this is really important to you.

JUNE

WORLD KNIT IN PUBLIC DAY

THE JOY OF KNITTING

Olympic Diver Tom Daley

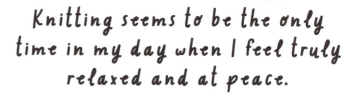

Knitting seems to be the only time in my day when I feel truly relaxed and at peace.

If someone had told me ten years ago that I would be writing about my love for knitting, I wouldn't have believed it! But it's taught me so many lessons: Firstly, how to be patient. It's something that you do over and over again, getting better at it all the time. Initially, I found it a bit tricky, as holding a pair of needles and getting the correct tension was tough, but practice makes progress. I've also learned that it's fine to make mistakes; even if it starts unraveling (or "frogging" as we call it in the knitting world), you'll get the chance to start again—and this time start from experience!

> *Nothing beats making something by hand, slowing down, feeling the fiber.*

You might have thought that knitting was for older people, but I assure you that is a stereotype that many knitters across the globe are trying to break down. Nothing beats making something by hand, slowing down, feeling the fiber, and my favorite thing of all is that everything I make is . . . MADE WITH LOVE!

Tom's Favorite Things to Knit

I wake up every morning looking forward to what I might be able to create that day, thinking about the many combinations of stitches, colors, and patterns. If you can picture your creation in your head, you can make it!

A SCARF FOR TEDDY

PURSE FOR YOUR COINS

WRIST WARMERS FOR A LOVED ONE

MENAGERIE OF CREATURES

You could sew pin backs or key rings to animal creations for an extra special gift, or string several together to make your own bunting!

JUNE

WHAT I USE TO KNIT MY FAVORITE THINGS:

Yarn   Needles   A pair of scissors   A sewing needle   A crochet hook

INTERNATIONAL FAIRY DAY

THE JOY OF FAIRIES

Writer and Actor Amelia Gann

You're never too old to believe in fairies.

As a child growing up in the countryside, I would walk to the bluebell wood in search of fairies. Sometimes I would leave them gifts like pebbles or wildflowers in a special corner of the garden and wait to see when they might be collected. I'd write letters to them, desperate to know all about their hidden world.

I'm still curious to know their secrets now, but unfortunately fairies are notoriously hard to track down. They make their abodes in quiet, uninhabited places like a babbling brook or an overgrown bramble bush. But if you wished to sit by a stream and while away the hours, you might just see a flash of a wing or sparkle of light. Believing in fairies opens us to a magical world of possibilities and reminds us to save a little sparkle of hope for that which is miraculous and unexplainable.

> *Believing in fairies opens us to a magical world of possibilities.*

Amelia's Brief History of Fairies

Fairies come in all shapes and sizes and are all over the world, bringing joy to those who believe in them.

A fairy is a type of MYTHICAL BEING. What a fairy is and what it is called in each culture is different.

The word *fairy* is derived from the Latin word *fata*, meaning FATE, as people believed that fairies had the power to enchant and change a person's destiny.

In ancient sources fairies are seen as minor spirits that delivered messages from GODS AND GODDESSES to humans.

In many cultures fairies are said to CAUSE MISCHIEF and are closely attached to nature, whether living in natural habitats or taking on the form of animals.

Do you have a fairy-like figure in your own culture?

INTERNATIONAL JOKE DAY

THE JOY OF LAUGHTER
Comedian Julian Clary

"Laughter is the best medicine" is an old-fashioned saying... and it's true!

You always feel better after a good laugh. And the only thing that beats a good, hooting guffaw is being the person responsible for it. Standing on stage in a packed theater, or even just amongst a group of friends, and saying something funny fills me with joy like nothing else. People look ecstatic and happy when they laugh and it's all because of me.

It's no coincidence that we say "make" me laugh: No one considers whether something is funny or not—it is an instant, instinctive reaction. A bit like crying, but the opposite. Laughter warms the heart and gladdens the soul. It's what I live for. It makes the world a better place.

> Laughter warms the heart and gladdens the soul.

How to Perform Stand-Up Comedy with Julian

Stand-up comedy is a show in which a comedian performs original jokes for a live audience. While these shows often feel like they're made up on the spot, a lot of preparation is involved.

GATHER MATERIAL
A good place to start is using your own experiences. All comedians have a point of view—their way of looking at the world. Express yourself!

THINK ABOUT WHAT YOU FIND FUNNY
Do you love sarcasm? Are you a fan of really bad "dad" jokes? Is slapstick your thing? If you enjoy your material, chances are an audience will, too.

WRITE YOUR JOKES
Think of jokes as a story—with a beginning (where you set up the characters involved and the setting), a middle (where you flesh out what is happening), and an end, or "punchline" (an unexpected twist).

THINK ABOUT YOUR DELIVERY
Pauses can be good for dramatic effect and to hold an audience's attention. Varying your pace will make the routine more interesting, going faster in some places and slower in others. Consider facial expressions and tone as well.

REHEARSE
It's a good idea to practice your act in front of other people so you gain confidence and learn how to pause for laughs. But don't memorize it like a script; you want your routine to feel conversational and natural, like a friend telling you a funny story.

NATIONAL JAM DAY

THE JOY OF MAKING JAM

Paulus the Cabaret Geek

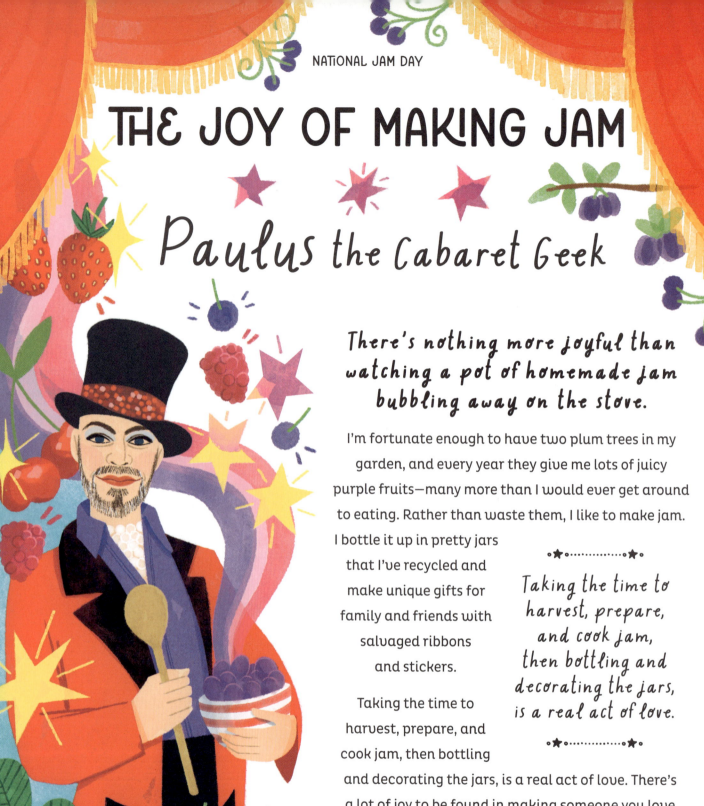

There's nothing more joyful than watching a pot of homemade jam bubbling away on the stove.

I'm fortunate enough to have two plum trees in my garden, and every year they give me lots of juicy purple fruits—many more than I would ever get around to eating. Rather than waste them, I like to make jam. I bottle it up in pretty jars that I've recycled and make unique gifts for family and friends with salvaged ribbons and stickers.

> *Taking the time to harvest, prepare, and cook jam, then bottling and decorating the jars, is a real act of love.*

Taking the time to harvest, prepare, and cook jam, then bottling and decorating the jars, is a real act of love. There's a lot of joy to be found in making someone you love smile. Plus, you're also bottling a little piece of late summer magic, which will brighten up your day when you pop it open and enjoy the sweet, luscious taste. Yum!

Paulus's Guide to Making Jam

I love reusing and repurposing everything I can, and making jam is the perfect way to do that!

! Ask an adult to help you when you're in the kitchen.

INGREDIENTS
- 4 pounds plums, pitted and roughly chopped
- 3/4 cup water
- 5 cups white granulated sugar
- 2 teaspoons ground cinnamon
- 1 tablespoon lemon juice
- A pat of butter
- Clean glass jars

1. Put your plums in a saucepan and add 3/4 cup water. Bring to a simmer and cook for 10 minutes until plums are tender. Increase the heat and bring the jam to a rolling boil.

2. Add sugar, cinnamon, and lemon juice, then let the sugar dissolve without boiling. This will take about 10 minutes.

3. After about five minutes, spoon a little jam onto a cold saucer. Push the jam with your fingertip—if it wrinkles, the jam is ready. If not, cook for a few minutes more and test again.

4. Take jam off the heat and add the butter. Let the jam cool for fifteen minutes then ladle into jars and seal.

5. It's now time to decorate!

| Choose a small piece of brightly colored material to decorate your jar. | Cut into a circle about 1 inch wider than the lid's circumference using pinking shears. | Secure to the jar with a rubber band and tie a bright ribbon around it, covering the band. | Add a label showing the date the jam was made and what flavor it is. | If you're giving it as a gift, add a name tag, too! |

JULY

INTERNATIONAL DRAG DAY

THE JOY OF DRAG

Showbiz Star and Strictly Come Dancing Judge Craig Revel Horwood

I've loved dressing up since I was a young boy growing up in Australia.

We had a dedicated dress-up box that was home to various wigs, feather boas, old dresses, and other accessories for me and my sisters to be creative with.

I was always fascinated with drag and playing different characters. Singer Boy George from Culture Club was a real inspiration for me during my teenage years. I loved the fact that he'd bravely wear makeup in public and made no excuses for it. I wanted to be just like him—proud of who I am. Drag gave me the confidence to be myself and to discover who I am. I didn't know at the time, but the joy this shy little boy found in drag one day would one day allow him to live out his dreams on the worldwide stage of theater, film, and television.

> *Drag gave me the confidence to be myself.*

Craig's Brief History of Drag

Drag is the art of dressing and acting in an exaggerated way as another gender, usually as a form of entertainment.

People who perform as women are known as DRAG QUEENS, and people who perform as men are known as DRAG KINGS.

One of the earliest examples of drag was in SHAKESPEARE'S TIME (the late 16th century) when women were not allowed to perform on a stage. This meant any female roles had to be played by men dressed up as women.

In the early 20th century, one of the biggest drag stars was JULIAN ELTINGE, who was so convincing during his variety shows on Broadway and in the West End, he would remove his wig at the end to reveal his gender, and the audience would howl in disbelief.

UNDERGROUND DRAG BALLS took off in New York in the 1970s. These pageants involved competing in different drag genres to impress the judges for trophies and cash prizes. They became a safe space for queer people of color to express themselves freely.

In 2009 the first series of DRAG RACE aired and introduced a mainstream audience to the fabulous world of drag—hosted by Ru Paul…who started on the underground ball circuit in NYC!

JULY

INTERNATIONAL DAY OF FRIENDSHIP

THE JOY OF A TEAM

Soccer Player Joanie Evans

The roar of the crowd fades away when I'm out there with my teammates.

It's just me and the girls: a symphony of cleats pounding the soccer field. We've practiced this play a thousand times, yet the joy of a perfectly timed pass to a streaking forward, the trust in their run, is ever-fresh.

You always feel like you belong and have a purpose when you are part of a team, especially one as amazing as the Hackney Women's Football Club. The friendships I formed throughout my soccer journey have given me the confidence I always dreamed of having, but never believed I would have. And it's the unwavering support from the teammates beside me that brings the most joy, the knowledge that they'll celebrate my goals and lift me up after a miss. That's the magic of friendship on the field. It's a bond forged in sweat, grit, and the shared passion for the beautiful game.

> The friendships I formed throughout my soccer journey have given me the confidence I always dreamed of having.

Joanie's Guide to Being a Good Teammate

Soccer players look out for one another. Here's how to be a good teammate when playing the game:

BE SUPPORTIVE
Soccer's a team sport, and the best teammates understand that. Celebrate your victories together, but also pick each other up after losses. Focus on contributing your best, not hogging the glory.

COMMUNICATE
Talk on the field! Guide your teammates with shouts and signals. Listen to their calls and adapt your play. Clear communication makes the beautiful game even more beautiful.

PRACTICE
Arrive on time, ready to work hard. Master your drills and understand your role in the team's strategy. A prepared teammate makes the whole team stronger.

ENCOURAGE OTHERS
Mistakes happen. Instead of pointing fingers, offer encouragement. A positive attitude lifts everyone's spirits and keeps the team focused.

TAKE IT OFF THE FIELD
Support your teammates outside of practice. Cheer them on at other games and celebrate their individual successes. True teammates have each other's backs, always.

JULY

NATIONAL PLAYDAY

THE JOY OF PLAY
YouTuber and Author Calum McSwiggan

When I was younger, I had a fear of growing up. I worried about the day I'd become a boring grown-up and forget the joys of being a child.

That's why, no matter how busy I get, I always try to find the time to embrace the magic of all the little things I used to love . . . and still love today. I love playing video games, or with Lego, or getting my friends together for a giant game of capture the flag. I love the crunching sound of the scoop as I dig into a bin at the candy store, the flashing lights of the fairground, and Saturday morning cartoons.

> I love the freedom that comes from play.

Sometimes life can get a bit sad and stressful, and that's when it's important to remember to laugh and enjoy yourself. I love the freedom that comes from play and exploration. I love the joy in the act of being silly, and the simple happiness that comes from having fun.

Calum's Play List

Childhood is magical. You may find yourself busy when you're older, so take the time to enjoy being a child. You could:

BUILD A FORT

GO ON A BUG HUNT

VISIT A THEME PARK

FIND A FOSSIL

FLY A KITE

BAKE A CAKE

PUT ON A PLAY

PLAY A VIDEO GAME

WRITE A STORY

CREATE CHALK ART

AUGUST

WORLD CALLIGRAPHY DAY

THE JOY OF HAND-LETTERING

Designer Jae Lin

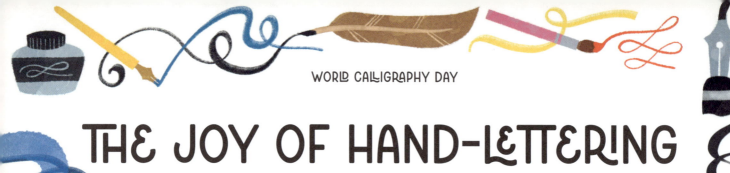

I love making words look as beautiful as they feel.

Growing up, I loved doodling my favorite song lyrics into my notebooks. Later, I started collecting quirky quotes, passages from books and positive affirmations—all compiled into a list of doodle inspiration. Eventually, I found out this type of art was called hand lettering, and I started trying all sorts of brushes, pens and markers to make different shapes and styles.

I'm drawn to quotes that give me hope.

It felt good to visually infuse these words that mean so much to me with the emotion that they make me feel.

When I started to draw phrases about being proud of my queer and trans identity, it felt powerful to show it to the world in bold, beautiful letters. These days, I'm drawn to quotes that give me hope from people who fight for a better world. Art, stories, and songs play an important role in helping us imagine and believe in the possibilities of change.

Jae's Hand-Lettering Mood Board

There are so many ways to make art with letters by hand! Grab something to draw on and something to draw with, and see if you can jump off from any of these ideas in order to create something of your own.

CHOOSE A SINGLE LETTER. Draw it big. Add doodles and details inside and around it. Give it a personality.

Got a song stuck in your head? Draw your FAVORITE LINE OF LYRICS in the way that it makes you feel.

Start with a few big shapes. Then, fill them in with WORDS THAT GO TO THE EDGES.

Come up with three different ways to write YOUR NAME.

Draw some letters FAR APART. Draw some really CLOSE TOGETHER.

Think of two CONTRADICTORY FEELINGS, THOUGHTS, OR SENTIMENTS. Draw one in one direction, then turn it upside down and draw the other one.

Make a letter or word THREE-DIMENSIONAL.

What makes you feel POWERFUL, WORTHY, OR WONDERFUL? Whatever images, words, symbols come to mind, put them together.

AUGUST

NATIONAL DOG DAY

THE JOY OF MY DOG
Casting Director Robert Sterne

My dog, Harry, is my pride and joy.

Harry has taught me how to treat other living creatures and although he'll never speak a single word to me, I've learned exactly what he is thinking and feeling in every situation (and vice versa). Every morning I am greeted by extraordinary wagging enthusiasm, and stepping out for a daily morning walk brings health, energy, and happiness to us both.

I live in London, where people are often in a rush. But if I walk down a street with Harry then people will stop and talk. Having a canine pal is a big responsibility: You mustn't leave them on their own for long periods of time, daily exercise is essential, and they can smell like your dirty socks if you don't give them a regular bath. But the responsibility of having Harry ends up being a big part of the joy of it, and in return Harry has become an endless source of unconditional love: My best friend, loyal and true.

Harry has become an endless source of unconditional love.

Robert's Reasons for Dog Ownership

Unconditional love. Devoted companionship. Constant entertainment. Life is better with a dog. But is that knowledge based on a feeling—or is there science at work?

IT'S A GOOD DEED
Some dogs have had a sad start in life and are looking for a second chance. By adopting, you are giving a dog a safe and loving home.

DOGS LIFT OUR MOOD
When we share eye contact with our dogs, oxytocin is released in our brains. Oxytocin makes us feel good!

DOGS MAKE US MORE SOCIAL
Walking with a canine companion can make us more approachable and give people a conversation starter.

DOGS HELP US IF WE'RE ANXIOUS
Even just petting a familiar dog lowers blood pressure, heart rate, slows breathing, and relaxes muscle tension.

DOGS ENCOURAGE US TO MOVE
Dog owners spend nearly 300 minutes every week walking with their dogs. That's 200 more minutes walking than people without a dog!

NATIONAL BEACH DAY

THE JOY OF A BEACH WALK

Charity Executive Mark Russell

There is something magical about walking along a beach . . .

Feeling the sand beneath your feet and listening to the wonderful sound of the sea and the waves lapping on the shore. Whether I go in the summer and walk barefoot with the sun on my back, or in the winter when I'm wrapped up warm and the wind and waves blow around me, when I'm on the beach I feel an overwhelming sense of peace.

To stand on a beach, to watch the waves, listen to the seagulls, and just take in the surroundings is one of the best ways I know to relax, and it brings me so much joy. Sometimes problems can feel really big, but standing on a beach I always find perspective and remember that whatever I face will get easier and life will get better. The timeless sounds of the beach remind me that my life matters and all will be well.

When I'm on the beach I feel an overwhelming sense of peace.

Mark's Beach Scavenger Hunt

The beach is the perfect place for a scavenger hunt. Here are a few things you could try to find.

GULLS
Remember to look up and you're certain to see a seagull, and you'll definitely hear them, too! Be careful though, seagulls are expert food thieves!

DRIFTWOOD
Driftwood is wood that has been washed ashore. It once might have been part of a tree, a building, lost cargo, or even the remains of a wooden ship.

PEBBLES
Pebbles are formed from rock that has been worn smooth by the water. You'll find lots of different shapes and colors—what's the most beautiful one you can find?

SHELLS
Empty seashells will often wash up on beaches, from all sorts of creatures that used to live in them. See if you can find at least four different shells, perhaps including a razor clam, common whelk, mussel, and common cockle.

SEAWEED
This should be easy—lots of seaweed gets washed up on the shore. There are many different types though, so see how many colors you can find!

STARFISH
You'll find these in tide pools or washed up on the shore after a rough sea. There are over 2,000 species, and they all have unique colors, shapes, and sizes. An amazing fact is that starfish can regenerate their own arms!

AUGUST

NATIONAL CINEMA DAY

THE JOY OF INDIAN CINEMA

Actor Seyan Sarvan

The Indian films that have my heart are tales of love, bravery, hope, and the perseverance of good.

And by good, I mean light breaking into the most unimaginable of places. No one expects the beautiful lotus (India's famous flower) to grow from muddy waters, but nonetheless, the lotus defies all odds and breaks through barriers that are presented to it so that it can bloom. Hope and light in the unlikeliest of places is what makes Indian cinema great to me.

I remember watching one of my first Indian films at the age of nine: I sat in front of a small TV screen, eagerly waiting for the movie to begin, with a bowl of Gulab Jamun (a delicious Indian dessert, which resembles a golden doughnut) on my lap. Immediately, I was transported to another world through song and dance, and was given the faith to believe that my dreams could come true.

Indian cinema gave me the faith to believe that my dreams could come true.

Seyan's Film Club

Indian films feature high production values and breathtaking visuals. Here are just a few of my favorites. These recommendations are rated G or PG, so they're suitable for you, but always check with an adult first.

MOTHER INDIA
Released: 1957

Directed by Mehboob, the central character is a village woman who is struck by poverty and upheaval, played by Nargis, who in my opinion is one of the greatest actors to have ever lived. The character faces testing times without compromising her truth, becoming a symbol of India's own pride as an ancient country and a new democracy.

In the following three films, NARGIS teams up with RAJ KAPOOR—another great Indian actor—whom we see playing characters from underprivileged backgrounds who have dreams that are not supported by society's view of them. Nonetheless, his characters persevere and find peace within themselves' that leads them to find peace in the world around them.

AWAARA
Released: 1951

Kapoor plays a man who becomes a criminal due to his tough life, but after meeting the character of Rita he tries to reform himself for love.

SHREE 420
Released: 1955

Kapoor plays an innocent village boy who comes to Mumbai with a dream to become successful in his chosen career. However, in order to survive he trades his morals for money.

MERA NAAM JOKER
Released: 1970

Directed, edited, and produced by Kapoor, this film is about a clown in a circus who makes his audience laugh at the expense of his own sorrows.

SEPTEMBER

WORLD GRATITUDE DAY

THE JOY OF SMALL MOMENTS

Entrepreneur Kortney Ziegler

Joy doesn't just come from the big, exciting things that happen in life.

My greatest joy derives from the small, but hugely cherished moments I'm able to spend with my wife and son. Immersing ourselves in family activities such as days out, game nights, or even times when we all help with homework, I see how we are cultivating an unbreakable bond through our shared memories.

My family stands as the bedrock of my happiness—an unshakable haven where there is love, laughter, and safety. By being present in the moment and practicing gratitude, everyone is able to appreciate the little things that bring us happiness and enrich our lives. The moments of joy I experience because of my family enable me to truly live as my authentic self, finding the relentless inspiration to persist as a storyteller, impact creator, and an unwavering advocate for positive change.

> By being present in the moment and practicing gratitude, everyone is able to appreciate the little things that bring us happiness.

Kortney's Guide to Finding Joy in Small Moments

Sometimes we are so focused on the big things in life that we forget about the smaller moments. Here are a few things you can do to appreciate the little things:

PRACTICE GRATITUDE
Things go wrong for everyone sometimes, so it's useful to remind yourself of all the good things in your life. Make a list of everything you have to be grateful for—whether it's the love of your dog, having a place to call home, or a good friend you can talk to.

BE PRESENT IN THE MOMENT
This might sound silly, because of course you're present in any moment, right?! But the truth is, our minds are often occupied thinking about that homework we've got or an argument with a friend. Whatever you're doing, try to focus on the here and now.

BE KIND TO YOURSELF
Treat yourself like you're your own best friend! Instead of beating yourself up when something goes wrong, run yourself a nice, relaxing bath, listen to some music, or make yourself a tasty snack. Go on! You deserve it!

BE KIND TO OTHERS
Being kind makes us feel happier—and there's even science to prove it! It also helps make the world a better place and creates the opportunity for new friends. Try to do at least one kind act a day, whether it's helping a friend, doing the dishes without being asked, or doing something for charity.

SEPTEMBER

NATIONAL COMIC BOOK DAY

THE JOY OF DRAWING COMICS

Cartoonist Lewis Hancox

When all my friends were using the playground to play, you'd find me, pen in hand, dreaming up a comic.

I was born a girl but always knew I was a boy inside, which was tough. I remember attending a primary school disco when I was eight years old with boys on one side and girls on the other, and feeling a deep sense of not belonging in either group. I found a teacher and requested somewhere quiet to sit—plus a set of colored pens and a stack of paper. While the other kids partied on, I spent the evening in the headmistress's office, drawing my first cartoon.

> I use cartooning as a kind of diary, a way to tell my own life stories.

Creating cartoon worlds was my way to escape the real one. I started out drawing cat and mouse capers, inspired by old Hanna Barbera cartoons like *Tom & Jerry* and *Scooby Doo*. Nowadays, I use cartooning as a kind of diary, a way to tell my own life stories, and to help other people like me who have felt different. It's helped me work things out and find my happy place, my friendship circle, and most important, find myself!

How to Draw a Comic Strip with Lewis

Drawing comics helped me through the hardest of times—and it could help you, too! Here's how you can get started:

FINDING YOUR STORY
This could be something real, entirely made up, or a mixture of the two! Whatever your story is, have a reason for telling it. Whether it's to make people laugh, think, feel something, or all of the above.

PLANNING YOUR PANELS
Decide how many boxes you want to tell your story in. I'd recommend starting with four evenly sized boxes in a row. Then you'll need to split your story up into the panels.

PLANNING—SPECIAL TIP
Your first panel should set the scene, so the reader understands the situation the characters are in. The last panel is where the punchline is—the last line of the joke, the twist, or the point you want to make. If you decide on what these two panels are first, then the middle ones are just filling in the gaps!

SKETCH IN PENCIL BEFORE PEN
Start by sketching your comic lightly in pencil. Rub it out and start again as many times as you like until it feels right. I always sketch my characters rough at first, starting with loose shapes. Then I make them neater with another line.

If your comic has words and speech bubbles in it, remember to leave room for them.

SPEECH BUBBLES
Speech bubbles are normally placed at the top, above the character's heads. You can get creative with how the words and bubbles look. For instance, if someone is shouting, make the words bigger and bolder.

PENNING IT IN
Once you're happy with your pencil lines, go over them with a pen. Take your time, and when you've finished and the ink is dry, rub out your pencil lines underneath. You can decide to leave the comic strip black and white or color it in.

HAVE FUN!
This is the most important tip! Something I've learned over the years is that it isn't about getting the drawings perfect, it's about telling a story. There's no good or bad, everybody has their own style. All you need for a good comic is an imagination.

SEPTEMBER

NATIONAL COOKING DAY

THE JOY OF COOKING
Theatrical Producer Cameron Mackintosh

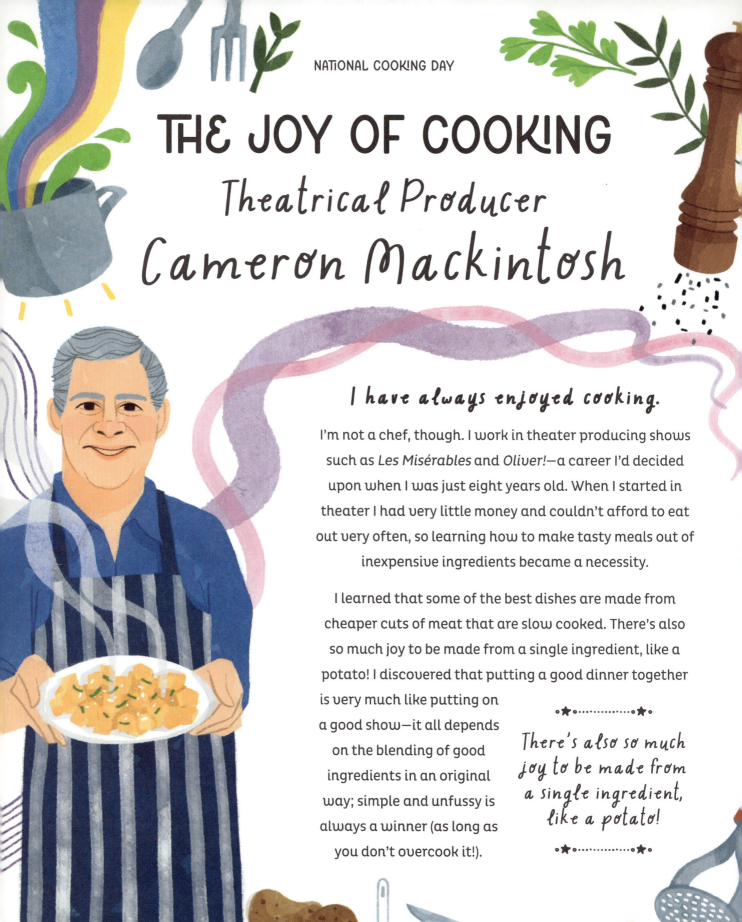

I have always enjoyed cooking.

I'm not a chef, though. I work in theater producing shows such as *Les Misérables* and *Oliver!*—a career I'd decided upon when I was just eight years old. When I started in theater I had very little money and couldn't afford to eat out very often, so learning how to make tasty meals out of inexpensive ingredients became a necessity.

I learned that some of the best dishes are made from cheaper cuts of meat that are slow cooked. There's also so much joy to be made from a single ingredient, like a potato! I discovered that putting a good dinner together is very much like putting on a good show—it all depends on the blending of good ingredients in an original way; simple and unfussy is always a winner (as long as you don't overcook it!).

> There's also so much joy to be made from a single ingredient, like a potato!

Cameron's Favorite Ingredient to Cook With: POTATOES!

Potatoes are a valued ingredient for their versatility . . . and flavor! There are so many ways to cook them. Let's boil, shake, and bake!

Ask an adult to help you when you're in the kitchen.

NEW POTATOES
You only need to boil new potatoes in lightly salted water for around 10 minutes. Test with a knife that they're done and add lots of creamy butter. Simple and delicious.

MASHED POTATOES
Once cooked, bigger, starchy potatoes are great for mashing, with a little salt, pepper, butter, and milk. Add a beaten egg to make it fluffier.

ROAST POTATOES
Toss cut white potatoes in some olive oil. Add herbs, salt, and pepper, and put in the oven at 425°F (220°C) for around 30 minutes, stirring about halfway through. Cook until really crispy on the outside (but still deliciously fluffy on the inside).

FRIES
The safest, healthiest, and cheapest way to cook them is in an air fryer if you have one (and far easier than using lots of hot oil). Just slice the potatoes into fries, add some seasoning, and leave them until they're golden brown and ready to eat.

SAUTÉED POTATOES
Peel, then chop the potatoes into smaller pieces. Parboil (partially cook) them but don't let them get too soft. Fry them in a pan with some chopped onion and chopped herbs until they're brown and crispy.

SEPTEMBER

WORLD TEACHERS' DAY

THE JOY OF TEACHING
Teacher Patty Nicolari

I find joy in creating a safe space for LGBTQ+ students and their allies.

When I was growing up in the 1960s in Connecticut, I always knew I was different than my three sisters, but I couldn't explain why. Later in middle school I realized I had crushes on my female friends. People would say to me, "Are you a lesbian?" and I didn't know what that meant.

It feels awful when you don't understand something and feel alone in your feelings—especially about being different. Different families were never even talked about in school or at home. For some reason, even today, this makes people uncomfortable. If I knew families came in different styles such as two moms or two dads, it would have helped me understand myself better. That's why, when I became an adult, I opened a school where students are celebrated for who they truly are. It's a wonderful experience to give children the opportunity to learn about true diversity and feel valued and respected.

> *It's a wonderful experience to give children the opportunity to learn about true diversity.*

3 Patty's PROUD Academy

I turned my negative experiences as a student into a powerful positive force. PROUD Academy is a safe and affirming school for LGBTQ+ students and their allies. Our students learn to:

SPEAK UP
LGBTQ+ students, allies, and teachers don't have to be silent about who they are anymore. Even if some people want us to be silent, we get to have a voice.

BE THEIR AUTHENTIC SELVES
We don't have to apologize for being different from others—that's what makes us all special. What do you think it would be like if we were ALL the same?

CONNECT WITH OTHERS
We take the time to learn about each other. The more we learn about our differences, the less there is to fear. How comfortable would you feel to go up to someone who may not be just like you and start a conversation?

FEEL PROUD
Students leave PROUD with a feeling of pride, knowing they will face challenges with confidence and take their rightful place in this world.

UNDERSTAND THEMSELVES
Our students learn about the history of LGBTQ+ people and different types of families.

Could you talk to one of your teachers and see if these are things you could champion in your school?

NATIONAL MUSHROOM DAY

THE JOY OF FUNGI

Environmentalist Isaias Hernandez

My joy is found on the forest floors in the wild and wonderful world of mushrooms.

When I connect with nature, I realize how many lessons there are, especially in the world of mushrooms. Mushrooms come in an astonishing variety, and they are everywhere. They aren't an animal, and they aren't a plant. They have their own kingdom and stand out in nature. I love how different and unique every single mushroom is, and yet they are all beautiful in their own way. They remind me that being different and unique makes me beautiful as well.

Mushrooms can stay connected even from miles away, which makes me think of my own community and how I stay connected with people in my life. They defy norms, and I do, too. Mushrooms remind me that beauty comes in all shapes and sizes, and I feel joy whenever I see one popping out of the ground. Next time you see a mushroom, make sure to say hi!

Mushrooms remind me that beauty comes in all shapes and sizes.

Mushrooms and fungi are truly incredible. However you must be careful as some are poisonous and can make you sick or even kill you.

Isaias's Anatomy of a Mushroom

Mushrooms belong to the fungi kingdom. We know they're living, so they need to consume energy and reproduce, but how does their anatomy allow them to do it?

CAP
The top part that protects the gills. It can look a bit like an umbrella!

SPORES
Teeny-tiny reproductive cells released into the air to produce new mushrooms.

GILLS
Spores are released from here to help the mushroom reproduce.

Not all mushrooms have gills—some have pores!

STEM
Supports the mushroom's cap.

MYCELIUM
Like a tree's roots, this underground network absorbs nutrients.

OCTOBER

WORLD FOOD DAY

THE JOY OF FOOD
Actor Miriam Margolyes

Since I was a little girl, I've been shamelessly greedy.

Always at the head of my list of treats is chicken soup. Growing up, first my mother plucked, then she boiled with carrots, onions, and celery. Slowly, a honey-colored, thick grease covered the soup. Then, it was cooled overnight, skimmed the next day, and served for lunch. Nothing ever in my life has matched its glories.

Another food I cannot live without is onions! I like them raw. I bite into their crunchiness like an apple and combine my bite with several slices of sharp cheddar cheese. Any kind of onion delights me. Spring onions, shallots, pickled, white, or red; my gnashers descend on their pungent, crisp flavor, and I am in a hot heaven. Few people admit to an onion frenzy; they say it makes their eyes water. That's exactly what I want. I really love strong tastes that call out in me a fierce response. Anything that makes me fart or squeak, any catch in my throat, any tingle of sharpness, and I line up for more!

> Nothing ever in my life has matched the glory of chicken soup.

Miriam's Recipe for Chicken Soup with Matzo Balls

Full of veggies, tender chicken, and moist matzo balls, this chicken soup is one of my favorite recipes.

INGREDIENTS

For the chicken soup
- 1 chicken with extra giblets
- 3 chicken stock cubes
- 1 bay leaf
- 4 carrots, sliced
- 2 onions, peeled
- 2 celery sticks, sliced
- 1 rutabaga, peeled and cut into chunks

For the matzo balls
- 1 ½ tablespoons fat from the chicken soup
- 1 egg, beaten
- ¾ cup matzo meal

METHOD

- Put the chicken in a large pot with the giblets and add enough water to cover the chicken.

- Once boiling, reduce the heat to a simmer. Crumble in the stock cubes and add the bay leaf and vegetables.

- Bring to a boil again, then reduce the heat to very low. Cover and simmer gently for 3 hours.

- Leave the soup to cool a little, then transfer to the fridge overnight.

- Once chilled, the fat from the soup will rise to the top. Save 1 ½ tablespoons for the matzo balls and set aside, then use a large spoon to remove as much as you can.

- Remove the chicken, shred all the meat, then add it back to the pan. Put the soup back on the heat and skim away any remaining fat while you bring it to the boil.

- Meanwhile, make the matzo balls by combining the fat, egg, and matzo meal. Stir into a paste, adding a little more water if needed, then chill for 10-15 minutes.

- Roll into about 12 small balls.

- Drop matzo balls into the soup for a few minutes, then serve.

INTERNATIONAL REPAIR DAY

THE JOY OF RESTORATION
Singer-Songwriter Will Young

I find a lot of delight in restoring old brass objects to their former glory.

I scour antique shops and flea markets and spot brass objects and ornaments and think to myself, *I can clean that up and bring it back to its former glory!* One of my favorite things to do is spend an evening cleaning my umbrella stand, my fire guard, door handles . . . you name it, it isn't safe from a good polish! It brings such immediate joy because the cleaning process presents such an obvious change from the starting place of darkened tainted metal to a gleaming shiny object which sings out in whatever room it is placed.

In a world where everyone wants the latest gadgets and flashiest phones, restoration reminds me of the value of the things we already own, and how, with a little care, previously unloved objects can quickly become beautiful.

> *Restoration reminds me of the value of the things we already own.*

Will's Advice for Cleaning Brass and Restoring Shine

Brass can lose its shine over time as oxygen causes it to tarnish. Luckily, you can bring the shine back with some simple homemade solutions!

INITIAL CHECKS
First, check the object is solid brass. Many items are brass plated, and these cleaning methods could damage them. Check the metal with a magnet: If it sticks, it isn't pure brass.

SAFETY FIRST
Test a small, inconspicuous part first to be extra careful. And always ask an adult before you begin.

THERE ARE LOTS OF DIFFERENT—AND FUN!—WAYS TO CLEAN BRASS.

WITH KETCHUP
Yep, it's true! Use a squirt of your favorite burger topping on a cloth and rub it all over the surface. Leave it for a few seconds, wipe off with a damp cloth, and buff dry.

WITH LEMON
Mix together some lemon juice and baking soda. Rub the mixture over the brass, buff away the grime, and then rinse off and dry with a fresh cloth. This will cut through the tarnish, but don't leave it on too long!

WITH TOOTHPASTE
Cover the brass in a thin layer of toothpaste and leave it for a few minutes before polishing with a clean cloth. Rinse with cold water and then dry.

OCTOBER

WORLD SWIM DAY

THE JOY OF SWIMMING
Actor Emma D'Arcy

For most of my life, I didn't like swimming. I'd take a quick dip in the ocean on vacation, but I much preferred being on dry land.

Then, a few years ago, something changed. I started swimming in an outdoor pool. There were lifeguards, and I used a float—I felt safe and brave enough to try. The water was cold and sent a great shock through my body. When I got out I felt elated! My skin tingled.

Over time, I discovered that swimming is about rhythm of the body and the breath. It's like a moving meditation. It clears my mind and relaxes me. And I feel so free in the water! I can make huge gestures with my body—reaching out as far as possible with my arms and kicking powerfully with my legs. Sometimes, I dream of swimming! Swimming has taught me a great lesson: Sometimes, you can turn a scary thing into one of your greatest joys.

> The water was so cold and sent a great shock through my body. When I got out I felt elated!

Emma's Guide to Swimming

I swim in different ways on different days! Here are a few things to try while you're swimming—and before you take the plunge make sure you get lessons from professionals, and only get into water supervized by lifeguards!

Think of your favorite song! Can you "play" the song in your head while you swim? Can you time your swimming to its rhythm?

Try making your strokes as big as possible! Enjoy being creative, owning the space, and making huge gestures with your arms and legs.

Think about different parts of your body. Notice the shapes your hands make as they cut through the water. Try tensing your stomach to stabilize your body or focus on the power of your legs.

What does it sound like underwater? Can you hear anything underwater that you can't hear above?

OCTOBER

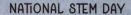

NATIONAL STEM DAY

THE JOY OF SCIENTIFIC DISCOVERY

Scientist Biswajit Paul

Scientific research is all about the joy of learning and understanding the world around us and inside of us.

Scientists are like explorers who gather information, run tests, travel to faraway places, and share what they have found. Difference and variety are very important to science. Imagine what would happen if all scientists were the same. We would all see things the same way, think about things the same way, and care only about certain things.

There are many kinds of scientists, and that's why it's fantastic that scientists live all over the world, speak different languages, and think different ideas. In the world of science, being different is a superpower. It helps us learn more, cure diseases, create new technologies, and work together to make our planet a better home for everyone.

In the world of science, being different is a superpower.

Biswajit's Guide to the Tiny Adventurers Inside Our Bodies

Do you know that inside our bodies there's an almost magical kingdom of cells containing DNA, genes, and chromosomes, that all work together to make you . . . you!

LEVEL 1: THE BUSY LITTLE CELLS

Some CELLS help you breathe. Some cells help you see. And some cells help you run and play. Some cells fight off illness like colds or flu.

LEVEL 2: THE DNA TREASURE MAP

Cells can do their jobs because inside each cell is a set of instructions, like a treasure map, called DNA. DNA molecules tell a cell what to do, and they are carried in structures called CHROMOSOMES.

LEVEL 3: THE ENCHANTED POWERS (GENES)

Part of DNA is a specific set of instructions just about you, called your GENES. Genes give each cell their own superpowers; they help tell cells whether you'll be tall like a giraffe or have teeth like a lion!

NATIONAL HIKING DAY

THE JOY OF URBAN HIKING

Professor Myeshia Price

There's nothing I enjoy more than exploring a city on foot.

I have lived in nine different cities and visited dozens. There is no better feeling than starting a day of city exploration with no destination, no map, no trails—with nothing but an open mind and a sense of adventure. Who needs mountains when you've got city steps?

My previous job as director of research at The Trevor Project, a suicide prevention organization for LGBTQ+ young people, and my current work in this area, is rewarding, but can it weigh heavily on my mind. When I'm urban hiking, I'm able to fully ground myself in the present, even if it's using the sound of cars whizzing by or music blaring from someone's window. Whatever it is, whether it's the smell of local cuisine in the air, or the feel of cobblestones under my feet, urban hiking helps me to reconnect with my surroundings.

> Who needs mountains when you've got city steps?

Myeshia's Guide to Urban Hiking

Urban hiking is making the most of urban spaces by hiking along city trails, paths, and bridges. Here are my top tips to help you explore:

OPEN YOURSELF UP
Part of the charm of an urban hike is having a sense of adventure and discovering new things. Whether you prefer a set route or just to wander freely, if you approach it with the right mindset you can't go wrong.

BE (SOMEWHAT) PREPARED
You won't need fancy gear, but you probably want to have the right kind of shoes. Bring water with you and go to the toilet before you leave if you're not sure about access to public spaces. Charge your camera for fun pictures, too!

INVITE OTHERS
The great thing about urban hiking is that different age groups can do it together in whatever way, and at whatever pace feels best for them—perhaps you can go with your grandma or a younger sibling!

KEEP YOUR EYES AND EARS OPEN
The entire point of an urban hike is to use the existing urban environment as your playground, so take it all in. While it can be more strenuous than a walk around your neighborhood, it's also a great opportunity to discover more, and you can't do that if you're not paying attention.

WORD TELEVISION DAY

THE JOY OF MAKING SHOWS

Director Amy Coop

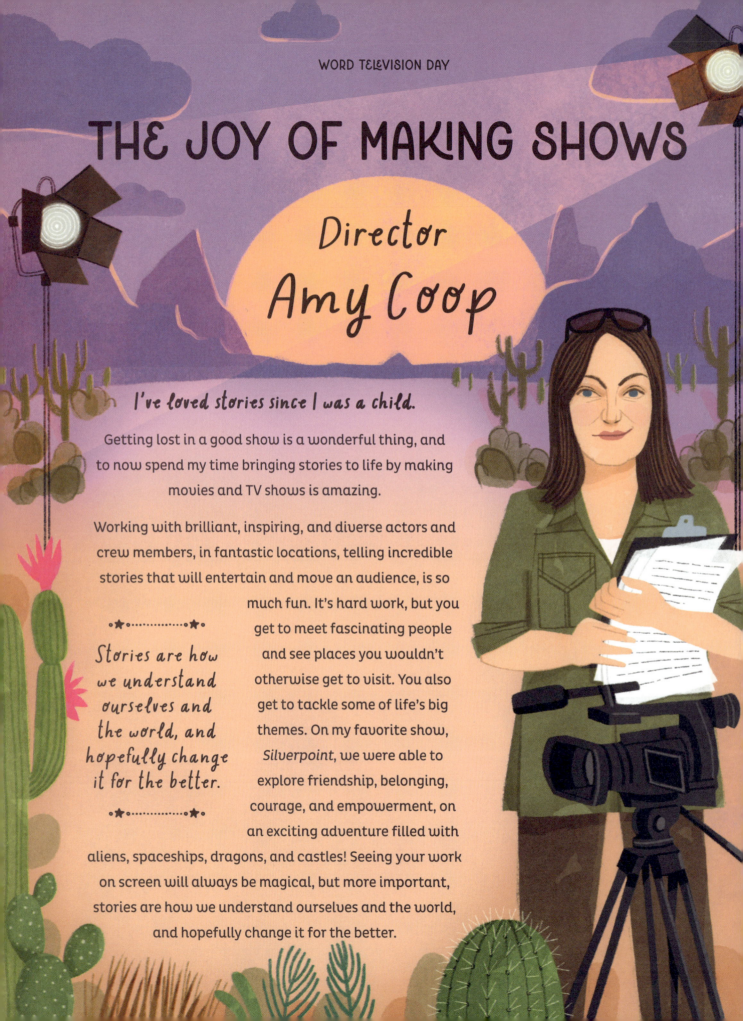

I've loved stories since I was a child.

Getting lost in a good show is a wonderful thing, and to now spend my time bringing stories to life by making movies and TV shows is amazing.

Working with brilliant, inspiring, and diverse actors and crew members, in fantastic locations, telling incredible stories that will entertain and move an audience, is so much fun. It's hard work, but you get to meet fascinating people and see places you wouldn't otherwise get to visit. You also get to tackle some of life's big themes. On my favorite show, *Silverpoint*, we were able to explore friendship, belonging, courage, and empowerment, on an exciting adventure filled with aliens, spaceships, dragons, and castles! Seeing your work on screen will always be magical, but more important, stories are how we understand ourselves and the world, and hopefully change it for the better.

> *Stories are how we understand ourselves and the world, and hopefully change it for the better.*

Lights! Camera! Action!
Amy's Guide to Making Your Own Show

There has never been a better time to make your own show. All you need is a phone, an idea for a story, and some friends to make it with.

WHAT'S YOUR STORY?
Think about the sort of stories you like and what kind of adventure you want your characters to go on. How does your story start? What's the challenge in the middle and where does it end? It might help to write a script for your story.

WHERE'S YOUR LOCATION?
What do you have around you as a place to set your show? Do you live near a park or the woods? Is there a skate park or an urban underpass? Does your mysterious uncle live in a haunted castle?

TAKE YOUR SHOT
Watch some of your favorite shows to see how they film a scene, then apply some of the practical ideas to your filmmaking. What kinds of shots do they use? Wide shots of landscapes or close-ups of faces? Medium-size shots of people or cutaways of important details?

The best way to learn is to do, so get out there and make your show . . . and maybe I'll see you on set one day!

NATIONAL ILLUSTRATION DAY

THE JOY OF DRAWING

Illustrator Ruth Burrows

Drawing has always been an important part of my life.

I spent most of my childhood playing with pencils, cardboard boxes, tape, and scissors, creating fantasy rooms for my cast of dolls to use as sets for their everyday dramas! I then went on to study theater design and realized that drawing could be used to tell stories and send messages—it can even help people make choices and change their minds about things.

Having illustration in my life has allowed me to be a very positive person. I feel joyful when I'm creating. I love using my drawings and positivity to help other people. When you draw a picture, you can give a voice to someone who might not be able to express their own feelings. Drawings have the power to cross borders and break down barriers—it's a visual language that everyone speaks!

> *I love using my drawings and positivity to help other people.*

Ruth's Guide to Drawing Emotions

One of my favorite things to draw is people. It's fun to draw them with different expressions. Try drawing these different emotions and see if your friends can guess what feelings you are trying to explain.

JOY
Eyebrows raised. Eyes looking up. Wide, open mouth smile.

LOVE
Head tilted down. Eyes looking up and to the side. Closed mouth smile.

SURPRISE
Eyebrows raised. Eyes wide. Mouth open in "oh" shape.

GRATITUDE
One eyebrow raised. Looking forward. Wide smile, mouth closed.

CONFIDENCE
Eyebrows straight. Eyes wide and facing front. Wide straight smile.

CALM
Face relaxed. Eyes gently closed. Neutral smile.

WORLD FOOTBALL (SOCCER) DAY

THE JOY OF SOCCER

Politician Mhairi Black

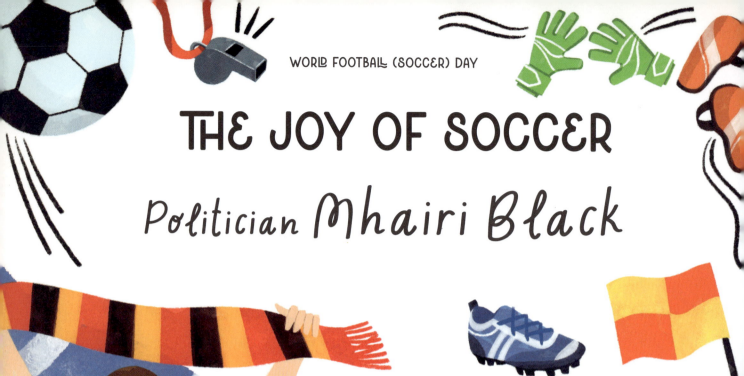

I grew up in a soccer-loving family, and we were all Partick Thistle fans.

When my brother and I were born, Dad took us along to soccer games just as my grampa did with him. Partick Thistle doesn't win as much as I would like, but it makes the games we do win all the more special. More than anything, I love spending the day with my family and singing along with all the other Thistle fans—some of the songs and chants you might hear include: "We're a Well-Known Glasgow Football Team," or "We Score When We Want." We sing to give encouragement to the best team in the world!

I love spending the day with my family and singing along with all the other Thistle fans.

It's also the best team because of its rich history of inclusivity. Since its inception, Partick Thistle, affectionately known as "The Great Glasgow Alternative," has welcomed players and fans from diverse backgrounds. The club continues to champion LGBTQ+ rights today and inspires me in my work as a Scottish politician and LGBTQ+ advocate.

Mhairi's Potted History of Partick Thistle

The club was formed over 140 years ago in Glasgow, Scotland, and has achieved a lot over the years.

Thistle played their first game on FEBRUARY 19, 1876. It was a 1-0 victory!

In 1995, Thistle became the first Scottish team to participate in the INTERTOTO CUP—a summer competition between European soccer clubs.

For the first fifty years, Thistle wore a blue uniform, but then a decision was made to change to the distinctive RED-AND-YELLOW STRIPES they wear today.

For the 2019–20 season, Thistle designed a new away uniform which featured a RAINBOW FLAG to show support for the LGBTQ+ community. They became the first Scottish club to do this.

Notable former players who have been inducted into the Scottish Football Hall of Fame include ALAN HANSEN, MO JOHNSTON, and ALAN ROUGH.

Thistle's mascot is a sun-shaped character called KINGSLEY, which was designed by artist David Shrigley.

DECEMBER

WORLD PANTO DAY

THE JOY OF PANTOMIME

Pantomime Dame Mama G

Pantomime can be enjoyed by everyone—just as long as you believe in magic!

If you've never been to a pantomime—or panto for short—it's a funny musical play that includes dance, colorful costumes, slapstick comedy, and audience participation. It invites you to believe in fairies, giants, magical forests, and that everything can be solved with a pop song and / or a custard pie! If you're a kid (or a kid at heart) it's the most fun ever!

> I've never lost my childhood sense of wonder when it comes to pantomime.

I've never lost my childhood sense of wonder when it comes to pantomime. Sure, I'm an actual grown-up (most of the time); but get me to a panto, and I'm as amazed as the five-year-olds who are seeing it with fresh eyes. I love that it gives me a chance to escape from a gray world into a land of glitter and laughter!

Mama G's Panto Guide

There are so many fun and fabulous characters in pantomime. Here are some of the typical ones you'll meet . . . and their surprising histories!

The FAIRY (yay!) always enters Stage Right and the VILLAIN (boo!) always enters Stage Left, because the Ancient Greeks thought that left-handed people were evil! *Dun, dun, duuuuuuun!*

The PRINCIPAL BOY, or hero, is traditionally played by a female-identifying actor in a short tunic. This was so that women could get around Victorian morality (because it didn't apply to men) and show off their lovely legs!

The DAME is normally a male-identifying actor "in skirts." This started when Shakespeare was writing plays because women weren't allowed on stage, so men had to play the female roles.

What do you shout when you see the GHOST? "It's behind you!" That's because in the 1700s a grumpy pantomime actor named Giuseppe Grimaldi was scared of death, and people teased him by making him think the Grim Reaper was—you guessed it—BEHIND HIM!

You could also be a PRINCESS, the COMIC, or even a HORSE!

What part would you like to play in a pantomime?

WORLD BASKETBALL DAY

THE JOY OF BASKETBALL

Basketball Player Abby Dunkin

Basketball has given me the chance to travel the world and meet so many different people.

The ability to play wheelchair basketball for Team USA is a dream come true. The thrill of representing my country at the Paralympics is unlike anything I've ever experienced before.

I've been so fortunate to share the basketball court with so many amazing players from around the world. I've always believed that life goes beyond the 90 feet of the court, and medals will eventually collect dust. The friendships I've been able to make along the way because of basketball mean so much more to me than any gold medal. The sport has given me a platform to share with others and advocate for acceptance and equality for all. Regardless of who you are or your abilities, basketball has a place for everyone.

> *I've been so fortunate to share the basketball court with so many amazing players from around the world.*

Abby's Guide to Basketball

These are the six moves you should know to play at the top of your game.

CROSSOVER
This is a dribbling move where you rapidly switch the ball from one hand to the other in front of your body. The aim is to deceive the defender and create space to shoot toward the basket or pass to a teammate.

BEHIND-THE-BACK DRIBBLE
A flashy move where the ball is dribbled behind your back. It can be used to change directions quickly or to surprise the defender.

LAYUP
A close-range shot typically taken after driving past the defender. It involves using one or two hands to place the ball gently off the backboard.

JUMP SHOT
A fundamental offensive move where you shoot the ball over a defender. This shot can be taken from anywhere on the court.

IN-AND-OUT DRIBBLE
A deceptive dribbling move where you fake going toward the defender with the ball (in) but then dribble back outside (out) your body.

HESITATION DRIBBLE
A subtle but effective move where you pause momentarily with the dribble, freezing the defender, thereby creating space to drive or pass.

CHRISTMAS

THE JOY OF PAWS
Singer-Songwriter Chet Lam

I once had a dream that I was surrounded by 100 Labradors on Christmas day. So many paws were cuddling me with such happiness and warmth.

Paws are so soft, fluffy and adorable. Yes, they are made for walking, as well as running, playing fetch, stretching, and high-fiving. But they're also perfect for tapping someone for more love and affection. What could be more joyful than that?!

> Paws are perfect for tapping someone for more love and affection.

I miss my Labrador, Leif. He passed away from cancer many years ago. He loved roaming free, and he always came back to me with the happiest smile. I know he's roaming somewhere now, and I know he will always save the biggest cuddles for me. I am sure we will meet again, though to me he's never gone. He opened up my heart, and that, to me, is joy. The love I had—and still have—for him has led me to living a happier, more peaceful, more compassionate life.

Chet's Paw-fect Guide to Holiday Cheer

Operation Santa Paws encourages animal lovers to share the gift of giving at shelters everywhere in December. Here's what you can do to join in:

PAWSOME DONATIONS
Ask your parents if you can donate some doggie goodies to the shelter. New toys, comfy blankets, or yummy treats will make the pups feel extra special.

BE SANTA'S HELPER
If you're old enough, offer to help at the shelter. You can walk the dogs, cuddle with the puppies, or even help clean their kennels (with grown-up supervision, of course!). Every bit of love and attention helps!

SPREAD THE WORD
Do you love taking photos of your dog? Ask your parents if you can take pictures of the shelter pups and post them online (with the shelter's permission). This might help them find forever homes!

DECK THE KENNELS
Make festive decorations for the shelter! Colorful paper chains or homemade dog treats in the shape of Christmas trees will brighten the pups' day.

The publisher would like to thank every person who shared their joy to make this book complete.

For Beau, Dolly, and Betty—my little bundles of joy. —S.J.G.

For Reem, all my love. —R.B.

The illustrations were created using gouache, ink, and digital media.
Set in Pluto, Rocking Horse, and Kindred.

Library of Congress Control Number 2024940961
ISBN 978-1-4197-7408-9
eISBN 979-8-88707-301-9

Cover © 2025 Magic Cat
Compilation and text excluding individual contributions © 2025 Simon James Green
Illustrations © 2025 Ruth Burrows
Book design by Kim Hankinson
Edited by Helen Brown

Individual contributions: Rebecca Root's text for National Bird Day © 2025 Rebecca Root; Paul Hawkins's text for International Flower Day © 2025 Paul Hawkins; Blair Imani's text for International Day of Education © 2025 Blair Imani; Nathan Jones's text for International Magicians' Day © 2025 Nathan Jones; James Aldridge's text for International Wetlands Day © 2025 James Aldridge; Stephen Fry's text for Global Movie Day © 2025 Stephen Fry; Dr. Clara Barker's text for International Day of Women and Girls in Science © 2025 Dr. Clara Barker; Rob Gillett's text for World Radio Day © 2025 Rob Gillett; Lauren Esposito's text for World Wildlife Day © 2025 Lauren Esposito; James Roesener's text for World Advocacy Day © 2025 James Roesener; Dr. Anand Patel's text for World Book Day © 2025 Dr. Anand Patel; Darren Styles' text for National Word Day © 2025 Darren Styles; Antonis Marquis's text for World Theater Day © 2025 AeJay Mitchell; Dr. Jo Hartland's text for World Health Day © 2025 Dr. Jo Hartland; Rina Sawayama's text for National Pet Day © 2025 Rina Sawayama; Dr. Ranj Singh's text for International Dance Day © 2025 Dr. Ranj Singh; Abby McElroy's text for World Veterinary Day © 2025 Abby McElroy; Matt Cain's text for National Tell a Story Day © 2025 Matt Cain; Andrew Moffat's text for Eurovision Song Contest © 2025 Andrew Moffat; Nancy Kelley's text for International Family Equality Day © 2025 Nancy Kelley; Hannah Breckbill's text for National Garden Meditation Day © 2025 Hannah Breckbill; Romolo Lanzi's text for National Train Day © 2025 Romolo Lanzi; Thomas Williams's text for Sherlock Holmes Day © 2025 Thomas Williams; Dòmhnall Idris's text for LGBT Pride Month © 2025 Dòmhnall Idris; Matthew Todd's text for World Environment Day © 2025 Matthew Todd; Tom Daley's text for World Knit in Public Day © 2025 Tom Daley; Amelia Gann's text for International Fairy Day © 2025 Amelia Gann; Julian Clary's text for International Joke Day © 2025 Julian Clary; Paulus's text for National Jam Day © 2025 Paulus; Craig Revel Horwood's text for International Drag Day © 2025 Craig Revel Horwood; Joanie Evans's text for International Day of Friendship © 2025 Joanie Evans; Calum McSwiggan's text for National Playday © 2025 Calum McSwiggan; Jae Lin's text for World Calligraphy Day © 2025 Jae Lin; Robert Sterne's text for National Dog Day © 2025 Robert Sterne; Mark Russell's text for National Beach Day © 2025 Mark Russell; Seyan Sarvan's text for National Cinema Day © 2025 Seyan Sarvan; Kortney Ziegler's text for World Gratitude Day © 2025 Kortney Ziegler; Lewis Hancox's text for National Comic Book Day © 2025 Lewis Hancox; Cameron Mackintosh's text for National Cooking Day © 2025 Cameron Mackintosh; Patty Nicolari's text for World Teachers' Day © 2025 Patty Nicolari; Isaias Hernandez's text for National Mushroom Day © 2025 Isaias Hernandez; Miriam Margolyes's text for World Food Day © 2025 Miriam Margolyes; Will Young's text for International Repair Day © 2025 Will Young; Emma D'Arcy's text for World Swim Day © 2025 Emma D'Arcy; Biswajit Paul's text for National STEM Day © 2025 Biswajit Paul; Myeshia Price's text for National Hiking Day © 2025 Myeshia Price; Amy Coop's text for World Television Day © 2025 Amy Coop; Ruth Burrows's text for National Illustration Day © 2025 Ruth Burrows; Mhairi Black's text for World Football (Soccer) Day © 2025 Mhairi Black; Mama G's text for World Panto Day © 2025 Robert Pearce; Abby Dunkin's text for World Basketball Day © 2025 Abby Dunkin; Chet Lam's text for Christmas © 2025 Chet Lam

First published in North America in 2025 by Magic Cat Publishing, an imprint of ABRAMS. First published in the United Kingdom in 2025 by Magic Cat Publishing Ltd. All rights reserved. No portion of this book may be reproduced, stored in a retrieval system, or transmitted in any form or by any means, mechanical, electronic, photocopying, recording, or otherwise, without written permission from the publisher.

Printed and bound in China
10 9 8 7 6 5 4 3 2 1

Abrams books are available at special discounts when purchased in quantity for premiums and promotions as well as fundraising or educational use. Special editions can also be created to specification. For details, contact specialsales@abramsbooks.com or the address below.

ABRAMS The Art of Books
195 Broadway, New York, NY 10007
abramsbooks.com